Cambridge Elements

Elements in the Philosophy of Søren Kierkegaard
edited by
Rick Anthony Furtak
Colorado College

KIERKEGAARD AND PHENOMENOLOGY

Kevin Hart
Duke University

CAMBRIDGE
UNIVERSITY PRESS

Shaftesbury Road, Cambridge CB2 8EA, United Kingdom

One Liberty Plaza, 20th Floor, New York, NY 10006, USA

477 Williamstown Road, Port Melbourne, VIC 3207, Australia

314–321, 3rd Floor, Plot 3, Splendor Forum, Jasola District Centre,
New Delhi – 110025, India

103 Penang Road, #05–06/07, Visioncrest Commercial, Singapore 238467

Cambridge University Press is part of Cambridge University Press & Assessment,
a department of the University of Cambridge.

We share the University's mission to contribute to society through the pursuit of
education, learning and research at the highest international levels of excellence.

www.cambridge.org
Information on this title: www.cambridge.org/9781009608947

DOI: 10.1017/9781009608916

First published 2025

A catalogue record for this publication is available from the British Library

ISBN 978-1-009-60894-7 Hardback
ISBN 978-1-009-60890-9 Paperback
ISSN 3033-4977 (online)
ISSN 3033-4969 (print)

Kierkegaard and Phenomenology

Elements in the Philosophy of Søren Kierkegaard

DOI: 10.1017/9781009608916
First published online: August 2025

Kevin Hart
Duke University

Author for correspondence: Kevin Hart, kevin.hart@duke.edu

Abstract: Is Kierkegaard a phenomenologist? Much depends on what we take "phenomenology" to mean, since the word has been stretched in all possible directions since Edmund Husserl wrote his major works. What have phenomenologists made of his writings? This question is easier to answer: He has been a constant reference point for many of them, although there is little agreement about his significance. This Element argues that he is a phenomenologist in the context of discovery, not justification. One finds attention to attunements in Kierkegaard, and one also finds modes of bracketing and reduction. Even so, his styles of thinking phenomenologically differ from those of most writers in this philosophical school. His phenomenology takes a *theological* path, one that leads from "world" to "kingdom," and one that often turns on what he calls "the moment."

Keywords: phenomenology, Kierkegaard, theology, European philosophy, acoustics

ISBNs: 9781009608947 (HB), 9781009608909 (PB), 9781009608916 (OC)
ISSNs: 3033-4977 (online), 3033-4969 (print)

Contents

... religiously, the only thing that matters is "how" ...

Kierkegaard, *NB* 22: 79

Introduction

This Element explores some of what happens when one allows the proper name Søren Kierkegaard to be associated with the word "phenomenology." It is not the first study to do so. Accordingly, I would like to acknowledge the pioneering work of Jeffrey Hanson, the editor of *Kierkegaard as Phenomenologist* (Northwestern University Press, 2010), Claudia Welz's thoughtful essay "Kierkegaard and Phenomenology" in *The Oxford Handbook of Kierkegaard* (Oxford University Press, 2013), and the editorial labors of Aaron Simmons and his associates in putting together *Kierkegaardian Phenomenologies* (Rowman and Littlefield, 2024). In an Element of this size, it is regrettably impossible to do anything like justice to the wealth of attunements that one finds in Kierkegaard's first and second authorships, and anything like showing a decent awareness of the many rich proto-phenomenological analyses he gives. For those things to be shown adequately, additional sections on love and sacrifice, along with evaluating alternate ways of construing Kierkegaard as a phenomenologist, would need to have been written, which would have drastically exceeded the limits set for this Elements series. The same limitations mean that next to no reference can be made to the texts in their original Danish. It has not even been possible to specify as narrowly as I would like the problems of even claiming Kierkegaard to be a phenomenologist. However, I have sought to identify several of those problems, see what eminent practitioners in the field have had to say about Kierkegaard as a possible forerunner, and sketch, all too briefly, what Kierkegaard's phenomenologies of the spiritual life and the Kingdom might look like if teased out more fully than he did himself. To that end, Section 3 turns on an unusual sense of reduction and Section 4 on a memorable conversion of the gaze.

1 Phenomenologies

If we are to make any sense of the conjunction "Kierkegaard and phenomenology" we first need to ask, "What is phenomenology?" The answer is nowhere near as simple as the question suggests.

As a placing shot, let's begin with Edmund Husserl (1859–1938), who is usually regarded as the father of phenomenology. Even here, though, we face difficulties, since Husserl's understanding of phenomenology developed very considerably over the course of his life. At first, he thought of the discipline as a way of clarifying concepts by tracing them back to their origin in our mental experiences. Slightly later, he revised his position: Phenomenology is not a description of psychic phenomena but a theory of essences with no adhesion whatsoever to empirical psychology. If we follow this revision of his theory, he believed, we could "go back to the 'things themselves,'" and so sidestep all prepackaged philosophical problems and think freshly.[1] We would avoid relativism and reductionism as well as psychologism. His concern henceforth was with how we can gain access to reality, which he thinks can happen by attending scrupulously only to what appears, or manifests itself, or gives itself, within its own limits. One must learn to "see" phenomena (even invisible ones) by eidetic abstraction, to clarify how they give themselves to us, and to distinguish layers of constitution.[2] His focus is on receiving the phenomenon just as it gives itself in intuition (awareness); and abiding by this commitment is what he calls following "the principle of all principles."[3] Phenomenology therefore isolates the essences of things, regardless of whether or not these things actually exist. I can be conscious of a golden ring or a golden mountain, and it makes no difference to their essences if the one exists and the other does not. Yet there are differences: Each gives itself in a distinct manner. The golden mountain cannot appear in perception but can in imagination. "Each objective region constitutes itself in accordance with consciousness," Husserl writes.[4] Two things are said here: Everything manifests itself according to its specific way of being, and all manifestations are linked to particular mental acts.

The task before us, Husserl thought, is to shift how we think about our mode of access to reality. It's not a question of uncritically correlating our thoughts with objects, according to the venerable formula for defining truth, *adequatio rei et intellectus*, which came to the schoolmen from Aristotle (384–322 BC) by way of Avicenna (c. 980–1037). Instead, the point at issue is matching our intentions with objects *as they are intended*. "Intention," here, means "consciousness of," not just volition, and includes many different mental acts, for instance anticipating, cognizing, desiring, imagining, judging, perceiving, and remembering, as well as willing. Inevitably, what is intended will have varying significance. The intentional object is what is intended exactly as intended, that is, as anticipated, cognized, desired, and so on. If I perceive my friend John, it is

---

[1] Edmund Husserl, *Logical Investigations*, trans. J. N. Findlay, 2 vols. (London: Routledge and Kegan Paul, 1970), vol. 1, 252. Husserl's rallying cry cuts across the calls of Neo-Kantians such as Hermann Cohen and Paul Natorp to "go back to Kant."

[2] See Husserl, *The Idea of Phenomenology*, trans. William P. Alston and George Nakhnikian (The Hague: Martinus Nijhoff, 1973), 46.

[3] Husserl, *Ideas for a Pure Phenomenology and Phenomenological Philosophy*, 1: *General Introduction to Pure Phenomenology*, trans. Daniel O. Dahlstrom (Indianapolis: Hackett Publishing, 2014), § 24.

[4] Husserl, *Ideas*, 1, 296.

very different from remembering him or imagining him in another place. In memory, John is not here in flesh and bone but merely represented: My intention can be at best only partially fulfilled. And in imagination, I cannot even posit John as existing in the past but must content myself with a quasi-perception of him. I imagine him in Oxford or Paris but my representation of him functions as if he were in Durham, NC, where I live. This "as if" is important, for my mental depiction of him abides in a "now" that falls outside the flow of time as I concretely experience it. We can already see that an intended object gives itself to me in a particular profile, depending on how I intend it. The human engagement with reality, then, is not one of merely responding to things regarded as simply existing; rather, it is a matter of aligning intentional objects with the objects that are intended and seeking adequate fulfillment.

In order for us to grasp the correlation of the subject's mental act and the intentional object (or, as Husserl calls them in *Ideas* 1 [1913], noesis and noema), we must therefore put naïve realism out of play. Most of the time we live in what Husserl calls the natural attitude, which is widely held but not the only stance that we can take with respect to the world about us. It's a mental framework that we associate with "common sense," which we variously inherit from Aristotle, John Locke (1632–1704), and Thomas Paine (1737–1809). The problem before us is less the distortions of reality that come from uncritically adopting the natural attitude, which, after all, has its uses when we know how it comes about, than in accepting the thesis that goes along with it, which insouciantly tells us that the intended object and the intentional object are exactly the same. This prejudice must be suspended – Husserl uses the Greek word ἐποχή (transl. *epochē*) – and only once this has been done can we be led back to the otherwise undisclosed domain of transcendental experience. In having access to this domain we do not thereby annul the existence of any object in the world; it remains just as it was. Only the thesis of the natural attitude is suspended. With this moratorium, which is perpetually willed by the philosopher, we can view the immense world of possible experience, of noetic–noematic correlations, which vary according to whether the intentions match intentional objects in consciousness, nature, or culture. Such is the effect of the phenomenological or transcendental reduction. It enables us to attend closely to how one experiences something, not the object that is experienced.

Husserl identified all sorts of stances we can adopt with respect to reality, not just the natural attitude. If I'm teaching physics, some of the time (depending on the level of students I have) I will be in the naturalistic attitude, regarding the universe as in effect a closed causal system. At other times, especially if I'm teaching an advanced class, I will be in the theoretical attitude, speculating about quantum theory or string theory, quite disconnected from the usual operations of cause and effect. At yet other times, I will be in the practical attitude, checking circuits and electrical leads, writing reports on experiments, and so forth. At home I might slip into the religious-mythical attitude in which I seek to account for the world and my place in it by appealing to the founding narratives of my culture. "Myth," here, does not mean a false story but a capacious, organizing narrative, what the ancient Greeks called μῦθος (transl. *muthos*), such as that of Creation, Fall, and Redemption. It can easily be seen that Husserl is animated less by the questions "What?" and "Why?" than by the question "How?" The interest is in the sense of the manner or way or being, not in "how" as an alternate way of asking "why?" (as in "how come?"). He urges us to see how things are in their modes of appearing, in every available human mental act, as well as in the various attitudes or stances we adopt with respect to the world. We are invited to pass from what is pre-given to what is given and, in the process, to wonder at the world and our place in it.

Not only did Husserl expand phenomenology by exploring definite fields such as time and imagination but also he kept probing the foundations of phenomenology and, in doing so, developing it in ever new directions. My consciousness, he realized, is not homogeneous; it has layers of sedimented sense that have built up over time and that undergird my experience of the world. I have understood the world by counting objects put before me, by trying my hand at various activities, by making judgments about states of affairs (and often revising them one or more times), and by imagining other situations. These are all active syntheses. In addition, though, I have benefited from passive syntheses, which occur primarily whenever my experiences as retained in consciousness associate with one another and, secondarily, when I pick up on experiences I haven't had but members of my family, church, workplace, or local community have had. All this cohered with Husserl's abiding interest in intersubjectivity, which finally, in his view, came to ground epistemic judgments. Such thoughts prompted him to pass from static to genetic phenomenology. As early as 1920, he also became deeply interested in what has since been called generative phenomenology, which turns on our distinct experiences of being at home and being in an alien place. Our recognition of a "home world" turns on our familiarity with community and local customs, language (including the narratives that are passed on from generation to generation), and shared values. Similarly, our awareness of an "alien world" stems from our experience of another community's generation of tradition and its distinctive language, accent, and idiom.[5]

---

[5] See Anthony J. Steinbock, *Home and Beyond: Generative Phenomenology after Husserl* (Evanston, IL: Northwestern University Press, 1995).

If we have read anything by Kierkegaard, we will quickly see that there is little that directly links him to what I've said so far about Husserl. To be sure, both philosophers prize experience, yet they approach it from quite different perspectives: The Dane thinks that we must make truth our own, possess it subjectively as well as acknowledge it as objectively so, while the German sees it as a way by which, through careful attention to phenomena, we might attain reliable epistemic judgments. Both are interested in human subjectivity, indeed psychology; but where Husserl is concerned to purify psychic acts, Kierkegaard seeks to describe definite mental and emotive states, such as anxiety, despair, guilt, and love, without severely reducing them to their a priori essences. One entertains the absurd, although this can easily be misunderstood. (Kierkegaard objects to Hegel's sense of reason as able totally to account for everything in reality and leaves open a space for that which is beyond reason.) The other insists on reason, indeed, on a teleology of reason that becomes apparent in the movement from the Greeks to the Germans. Kierkegaard thinks that "possibility is the weightiest of all categories," but his interest is in how anxiety is leagued with possibility whereas Husserl is fascinated by the endless possibilities of noetic–noematic correlation.[6] Is there any common ground between the two philosophers? In terms of their writings, only a little, perhaps *Repetition* (1843), where one finds an intriguing linking of experience and reflection, and in the area of ethics. As we shall see later, there may also be a shared orientation, although one not thematized by Kierkegaard.

Husserl wrote far less about ethics than Kierkegaard did. The German was committed to self-responsibility and especially to the renewal of the European mind which, he thought, had atrophied after World War I and, more, had lost faith in reason. He was skeptical about the empty formalism of Kant's phrasing of the categorical imperative, while nonetheless committed to the objectivity of values. Accordingly, he proposed a deflated version of the categorical imperative that depends on what one can reasonably do in one's sphere of action. In old age, however, he affirmed an ethics of love; and this would have appealed to Kierkegaard. The Dane would have found Husserl's idea of God as the "all-consciousness" somewhat chilly, though; it would have reminded him too much of German idealism and would have kept the believer in the sphere of "Religiousness A," in which one seeks to form oneself in this life by following an idea of God.[7] The high aim, as we learn in *Unscientific Postscript* (1846), is "Religiousness B," in which one

---

[6] Søren Kierkegaard, *SLW*, 11.

[7] See Husserl, *The Basic Problems of Phenomenology: From the Lectures, Winter Semester, 1910–1911*, trans. Ingo Farin and James G. Hart (Dordrecht: Springer, 2006), appendix XIII.

lives oriented to eternity, painfully riven by a conviction of sinfulness and the paradox of the singular God-Man, Jesus Christ.

More generally, Husserl writes philosophical papers and treatises, always imparting theories in a professorial voice to the academy at large, while Kierkegaard multiplies pseudonymous works in an effort to facilitate indirect communication, to make the reader judge a case or a situation for himself or herself. He writes, he says, for "that single individual whom I with joy and gratitude call *my* reader, that single individual, who willingly reads slowly, reads repeatedly, and who reads aloud – for his own sake."[8] This reader subjectively appropriates what Kierkegaard writes and puts it to existential use. Of course, this hope also applies to those works he writes above his own signature; he offers edifying discourses "with the right hand" while also offering the pseudonymous writings "with the left hand."[9] We know that Husserl had read and admired Kierkegaard, most likely in Christoph Schrempf's German translations (1890–1924), but it was the sort of respect that comes from an honest appreciation of a completely different approach to one's field. Besides, his exposure to the Dane's thought came far too late to influence his own writings.[10] Plainly, we must look elsewhere if we are to find a meaningful relation between phenomenology and Kierkegaard.

We might begin by looking back in history: While phenomenology was elaborated in a highly original and ramified manner by Husserl, he was not the first person to evoke it, at least in a preliminary way. Husserl himself thought that René Descartes (1596–1650) stumbled upon phenomenology, even on the reduction, but failed to make anything of either. He also set store by Immanuel Kant (1724–1804), who used the word "phenomenology" on several occasions and who developed in *The Critique of Pure Reason* (1781, 1787) a rich theory of the modes in which things appear to us. J. G. Fichte (1762–1814), whom Husserl likewise esteemed, proposed that the second part of the *Wissenschaftslehre* would be a phenomenology, "a doctrine of appearance and illusion."[11] We get a little closer to Kierkegaard (and further away from him at the same time) when we reach G. W. F. Hegel (1770–1831), if only because his polemic against Hegel – and Danish Hegelians such as Hans Lassen Martensen (1808–84) and Johan Ludvig Heiberg (1791–1860) – conceals certain debts to

---

[8] Kierkegaard, *UDVS*, 5.   [9] Kierkegaard, *WA*, 3.

[10] See Leon Shestov, "In Memory of a Great Philosopher: Edmund Husserl," *Philosophy and Phenomenological Research*, 22: 4 (1962), 461.

[11] J. G. Fichte, *The Science of Knowing*, trans. and intro. Walter E. Wright (Albany: State University of New York, 2005), 107. Also see Violetta L. Waibel, J. Daniel Breazeale, and Tom Rockmore, ed., *Fichte and the Phenomenological Tradition* (Berlin: De Gruyter, 2000).

him, perhaps not least of all to Hegel's notions of phenomenology and dialectic.[12] Phenomenology, for Hegel, has a dialectical structure, for consciousness experiences the world as it appears to it in progressively concrete ways.

On the face of it, Kierkegaard has a related dialectic of the aesthetic, the ethical, and the religious. *Stages on Life's Way* (1845), in particular, describes intersecting spheres of human existence, which shift in their mutual relations more than one finds in the forward thrust, neutralization, and retention of the *Aufhebung* (sublation) in Hegel's threefold philosophy of Idea, Nature, and Spirit. Doubtless Kierkegaard's use of dialectic answers more surely to Socrates than to Hegel; it's a matter of indirectly leading each reader by a process of maieutic questioning to a felt judgment about a concept or situation, not a dynamic unfolding of an objective state of affairs in logic or history. If we take a step back, we can see that his whole authorship is an extensive to-and-fro between various pseudonymous authors – Johannes Climacus, Anti-Climacus, Constantin Constantius, Frater Taciturnus, Inter et Inter, Quidam, Vigilius Haufniensis, and all the rest – and himself; and we, his readers, are challenged by all these different views of life and must find our own way through them in order to reach settled decisions about the issues he puts before us.

It is worth pausing to note Kierkegaard's final view of using pseudonyms. Thinking of the authorship presented over so many different signatures, he wrote, "I have actually been used without really knowing it myself, or knowing it fully. And now, for the first time, I understand and can see the whole of it – but then, of course, I cannot say 'I.'"[13] Philosophy, for Kierkegaard, is a putting on stage of many and varied characters concerned with questions and possible answers. We must be careful not to attribute ideas to Kierkegaard when they might better be attributed to one of his characters. All this is quite different from what we have come to expect in modern analytic philosophy in which we hear the reflections of a single individual, refined almost out of existence, who considers them from nowhere in particular.

If the prehistory of phenomenology is not of sufficient help to us, what of its developments after the work of the founding father? Phenomenology is sometimes described, tongue in cheek, as a church in which there is one Messiah (Husserl) and many heretics. Certainly, it is a broad church. Of

---

[12] For Kierkegaard's debts to Danish Hegelianism, see Jon Stewart, *Kierkegaard's Relations to Hegel Reconsidered* (Cambridge: Cambridge University Press, 2003). For a note of caution, see Thomas J. Millay, "Concrete *and* Otherworldly: Reading Kierkegaard's *Works of Love* alongside Hegel's *Philosophy of Right*," *Modern Theology*, 34: 1 (2018), 23–41.

[13] The line is taken from a scrap of paper written by Kierkegaard at the time of *The Point of View*. See Joakim Garff, *Søren Kierkegaard: A Biography*, trans. Bruce H. Kirmmse (Princeton, NJ: Princeton University Press, 2005), 559.

course, there are Husserlians of strict observance, but most of the better-known phenomenologists have disagreed with him about one or more things, including aspects of his approach to philosophy that he deemed fundamental, such as the primacy of absolute givenness, the importance of intentionality, and the revelation of transcendental life that comes from performing the reduction. Even when one or more of these terms is retained, it is not uncommon for them to be in a new configuration, which changes their significance and orientation. Perhaps one of these thinkers will give us an idea of whether Kierkegaard can reasonably be tied in to phenomenology and, if so, how. There are many of them, but I can consider only a handful of the more promising candidates for our concerns. At the very least, we shall get a sense of the limits of "phenomenology," if indeed there are any. In Section 2, I shall introduce other phenomenologists and consider their views of Kierkegaard and what they have made of him.

Undoubtedly, the most spectacular instance of an early deviation from the thought of the master is Martin Heidegger (1889–1976). At first, Husserl regarded the young Heidegger as his closest and most brilliant collaborator. "You and I are phenomenology," he would say in their early years of partnership.[14] By 1931, however, in a letter to Roman Ingarden (1893–1970), he would darkly refer to Heidegger (and Max Scheler) as "my antipodes."[15] In 1926, during their holidays in the Black Forest, Heidegger showed Husserl the manuscript of *Being and Time* (1927). Soon thereafter, Husserl discerned that the younger man was going in his own direction, seduced away from the truth, Husserl thought, by his residual Catholic "prejudices." (He had studied under Heinrich Finke [1855–1938] who had hoped to appoint Heidegger to the chair of Catholic Philosophy at Freiburg before changing his mind and supporting the apparently more reliable Josef Geyser [1869–1948].) Husserl asked Heidegger to read the draft of his article on phenomenology for the fourteenth edition of the *Encyclopedia Britannica* (1929), in the hope that, over the course of the exchange, Heidegger might be enticed to return to the fold. Collaboration became confrontation: The younger man's redrafting of the article exposed the increasing rift between them, and a careful reading of *Being and Time* by Husserl over the period of spring 1927 to fall 1929 showed that it was unbridgeable.

---

[14] Dorion Cairns, *Conversations with Husserl and Fink*, ed. Richard M. Zaner (The Hague: Martinus Nijhoff, 1976), 9.

[15] Husserl, *Briefwechsel*, ed. Karl Schuchmann with Elisabeth Schuhmann, 10 vols. (Dordrecht: Kluwer, 1994), vol. 3, 274.

What had happened? In *Ideas* 1 Husserl had patiently delineated both material and formal ontologies in his new, exacting methodology as a way of approaching being. Heidegger, however, had distanced himself from Husserl by stressing the ontological path to reality in preference to the epistemic one as the proper role for phenomenology. (Meanwhile, in the *Nachlass*, Husserl was sketching the inlaying of epistemic judgments in intersubjectivity, and so supplying an ontology as well as an epistemology.) Where Husserl would see reduction as uncovering the vast transcendental field of noetic–noematic correlations, Heidegger would summarily redefine it as a passage from beings to being.[16] More generally, where Husserl took pains to elaborate the constitutive-phenomenological clarification of the regions of being – the ways in which all phenomena show themselves, depending on whether they belong to consciousness, nature, or culture – Heidegger transposed the analysis into what Husserl took to be philosophical anthropology.[17] For Husserl, the important figure is the ghostly transcendental onlooker who is consequent on the reduction; for Heidegger, it is *Dasein*, the "being-there" of human being in concrete situations.

It is Heidegger, not Husserl, who allowed Kierkegaard to influence his thought. In 1923 Heidegger remarks in his foreword to his course "The Hermeneutics of Facticity" that impulses for his thought "were given by Kierkegaard, and Husserl opened my eyes."[18] Several years later in *Being and Time*, we are told that "The man who has gone farthest in analyzing the phenomenon of anxiety is Søren Kierkegaard"; and indeed the influence of *The Concept of Anxiety* (1844) runs far and wide through the book, more than Heidegger's brief note would suggest.[19] Similarly, Heidegger praises Kierkegaard for seeing "the *existentiell* phenomenon of the moment of vision," although he does not think that the Dane interprets it existentially in a convincing manner. As Heidegger sees things, Kierkegaard unduly restricts himself by appealing to the traditional categories of time and eternity.[20] Kierkegaard's thought thus remains at the level of particular beings rather than probing the truth (or meaning) of being as such. Moreover, Heidegger thought that the Dane remained "dominated by Hegel" as regards ontology and that the real philosophical force of his writings abides in his "edifying

---

[16] Martin Heidegger, *The Basic Problems of Phenomenology*, trans., intro., and lexicon Albert Hofstadter, rev. ed. (Bloomington: Indiana University Press, 1988), 21.

[17] Husserl, *Psychological and Transcendental Phenomenology and the Confrontation with Heidegger (1927–1931)*, trans. and ed. Thomas Sheehan and Richard E. Palmer (Dordrecht: Kluwer, 1997), 284.

[18] Heidegger, *Ontology – The Hermeneutics of Facticity*, trans. John van Buren (Bloomington: Indiana University Press, 1999), 4.

[19] Heidegger, *Being and Time*, trans. John Macquarrie and Edward Robinson (Oxford: Basil Blackwell, 1978), 492, 1.6, n. iv.

[20] Heidegger, *Being and Time*, 497, 2.4, n. iii.

writings."[21] Given that, for Heidegger, Kierkegaard stays on the level of ontic science while he himself ponders more profound ontological issues, it seems unlikely that the author of *Being and Time* can help us to discern a significant profile of the Dane as phenomenologist.

Somewhat before Heidegger's dramatic ascent in the competitive world of German philosophy, the Munich and Göttingen Circles, centered on Husserl – and, to some extent, Adolph Reinach (1883–1917) – were impressed by the realism of the new approach to philosophy signaled by the publication of *Logical Investigations* (1900–1) and "Philosophy as a Rigorous Science" (1910–11). Realism, here, is the claim that objects exist without any need for consciousness (although consciousness may well filter how we register them). Inevitably, these younger philosophers retreated from the master when he formulated the transcendental reduction. In particular, Ingarden rebelled against the innovation and dismissed what he regarded as the "fairy world" of transcendental life.[22] Hedwig Conrad-Martius (1888–1966), Edith Stein (1891–1942), and Gerda Walther (1897–1977) also accepted the realist understanding of the new philosophical school, yet all three diverged from Husserl in pursuing their deep and abiding interests in Christianity. This too was a breach with the master. In *Ideas* 1 Husserl insisted that God's manner of transcending the world requires that we bracket his very existence; besides, Husserl thought, the philosopher should be free, which includes independence with respect to Christian teaching. Only later in his limit-phenomenology did he countenance ways in which we might make out the very partial intuitions of the deity that some people receive.[23] That was detailed in the *Nachlass*, which saw the light of day only after Conrad-Martius, Stein, and Walther had each passed away.

So here, one might think, is a plausible opportunity to pair a phenomenologist with Kierkegaard so as to uncover at least an anticipation of phenomenology on his part, doubtless a religious inflection of it, one that might well asterisk the *Eighteen Unbuilding Discourses* (1843–44), Anti-Climacus's *Practice in Christianity* (1850), and other overtly Christian writings. Not so. Walther was entranced by the mystical thread that runs through Catholicism. Conrad-Martius, who was at home in liberal evangelical Christianity, also looked to mysticism, especially Jakob Boehme, when articulating her view of the qualifying source (*Quall*) in each of us that makes us what we are.[24] And Stein sought

---

[21] Heidegger, *Being and Time*, 494, 2.45, n. vi.

[22] Roman Ingarden, *On the Motives Which Led Husserl to Transcendental Idealism*, trans. Arnór Hannibalsson (The Hague: Martinus Nijhoff, 1975), 28.

[23] Husserl, *Ideas* 1, § 58. Also see § 51 Remark.

[24] See Hedwig Conrad-Martius, *Metaphysical Conversations*, ed. and trans. Christina M. Gschwandtner (Berlin: De Gruyter, 2023), 88.

a way to keep phenomenology and Thomism in dialogue. Yet although Kierkegaard's pseudonym Anti-Climacus is intensely Christian, and he himself barely less so, at least when imagining the Christian ideal, neither had any special interest in God as the most real of all essences (Conrad-Martius), apophatic spirituality (Stein), or mystical experience (Walther).[25] Although he had a keen awareness of the hiddenness of God, Kierkegaard seems to have restricted his prayer life to petitions and eucharistic devotions, and he leans heavily in the direction of Martin Luther (1483–1546), not Thomas Aquinas (c. 1225–74).[26] It is Luther who informs Kierkegaard's understanding of justification, while Aquinas's awareness of nature in its relations with Grace is far removed from Kierkegaard's.[27] Besides, he would have been skeptical about the systematic impulse behind the *Summa theologiæ* and the *Summa contra gentiles*, and there is nothing systematic about Luther.

I will return to one more German phenomenologist in a moment, but in order to give a decent appreciation of just how broad a church phenomenology is (or, if you prefer, how well it tolerates heresies), I wish first to look briefly at three modifications of Husserl's phenomenology that have come from France. The first of these is proposed by Emmanuel Levinas (1906–95) who studied with Husserl in Freiburg im Breisgau, participating in his last seminar on intersubjectivity, while also auditing Heidegger's seminars (1928–29). Returning to Paris, Levinas published *The Theory of Intuition in Husserl's Phenomenology* (1930), which served to introduce many French philosophers, including Jean-Paul Sartre (1905–80), to the new way of thinking, more so than Jean Héring's earlier *Phénoménologie et philosophie religieuse* (1925). What gripped Levinas is the Husserl for whom the meaning of human experience can be fully explicated by intentional analysis.[28] Toward the end of the book, however, he leveled two serious criticisms of the reduction. Here is the first. Intentionality presumes the anteriority and reality of the world; after all, consciousness is always consciousness of *something*, and this "something" transcends consciousness. Yet there are times when Husserl entertains the thought of a pure consciousness without a world (e.g., *Ideas* 1, § 49); and Levinas worries that the reduction is

---

[25] See Conrad-Martius, *Metaphysical Conversations*, Edith Stein, "Ways to Know God," trans. Rudolf Allers, *The Thomist*, 9: 3 (1946), 379–420, and Gerda Walter, *Phenomenology of Mysticism*, trans. Antonio Calcagno (Berlin: De Gruyter, 2024).

[26] For further discussion, see David R. Law, *Kierkegaard as Negative Theologian* (Oxford: Oxford University Press, 1993).

[27] See Jack Mulder, Jr., *Kierkegaard and the Catholic Tradition: Conflict and Dialogue* (Bloomington: Indiana University Press, 2010).

[28] See Emmanuel Levinas, "Questions and Answers," *Of God Who Comes to Mind*, trans. Bettina Bergo (Stanford, CA: Stanford University Press, 1998), 87–88.

precisely a leading back to transcendental consciousness which stands apart from the world.[29] Reduction would be therefore an abstraction. (Levinas may well have been influenced by conversations about the reduction that he had had with Eugen Fink [1905–75] which resulted in the latter's *Sixth Cartesian Meditation* [comp. 1932, pub. 1988].[30])

The second criticism is no less biting. Reduction seems to take us back to a solipsistic life, an individual consciousness that does not open onto the lived reality of other people. More than a reduction to a transcendental ego is needed, and at the time that *The Theory of Intuition* went to press (1930) Husserl had not yet published his settled views on an intersubjective reduction.[31] He went some distance in that direction, however, in the Paris Lectures, given at the Sorbonne in February 1929, in speaking of "an intersubjective transcendental community."[32] The lectures were expanded with Fink's help back in Freiburg, becoming the *Cartesian Meditations* (comp. 1931; German pub. 1950) and this German text was rendered into French by Gabrielle Peiffer and Levinas, a project overseen by Alexandre Koyré (1892–1964). The book appeared in Paris in 1931 and largely shaped the early reception of phenomenology in France. Yet the Fifth Meditation, on intersubjectivity, which Levinas translated, is beleaguered by ambiguities and hesitations; its talk of "analogizing appresentations" and "empathy" did nothing, in Levinas's view, to change his mind about Husserl's reduction as essentially a solipsistic act.

Levinas therefore develops phenomenology as intentional analysis without reference to the transcendental reduction. He insists that the other person cannot be turned into a phenomenon, and therefore be led back to my consciousness; instead, he or she is an enigma who imposes on me an unavoidable and irrecusable responsibility for him or her. Reduction is not thereby avoided, however. Eventually, in *Otherwise Than Being* (1978), Levinas proposes a reduction of his own, from the Saying to the Said. This does not manifest a "transcendental appearance," he says, but leads us back from what has been said, and therefore has entered the order of being, to the speaking person who risks vulnerability and openness in the first place.[33] I shall say something about how Levinas figures Kierkegaard in the following section. For now, though, it

---

[29] Later, Levinas will himself perform a thought experiment in which everything reverts to nothingness, which reveals to him the *il y a* ("there is"). See *Existence and Existents*, trans. Alphonso Lingis (Dordrecht: Kluwer, 1988), 57.

[30] See Eugen Fink, *Sixth Cartesian Meditation: The Idea of a Transcendental Theory of Method*, trans. Ronald Bruzina (Bloomington: Indiana University Press, 1995), esp. 120.

[31] See Levinas, *The Theory of Intuition in Husserl's Phenomenology*, 2nd ed., trans. André Orianne (Evanston, IL: Northwestern University Press, 1995), 150–51.

[32] Husserl, *The Paris Lectures*, trans. and intro. Peter Koestenbaum (Dordrecht: Kluwer, 1998), 35.

[33] Levinas, *Otherwise Than Being or Beyond Essence*, trans. Alphonso Lingis (The Hague: Martinus Nijhoff, 1981), 5.

suffices to see that while no one doubts that Levinas is a phenomenologist he does not follow Husserl with regard to one of the very things that the founding father of the discipline took to be essential: transcendental reduction. If there is any rapport between the Dane and the Frenchman, it is less likely to be in their settled views of ethics and religion, which, as we shall see, differ markedly, than in their views of love, which, in Levinas's case, comes late in his intellectual itinerary.[34] The closest parallel may well be, intriguingly enough, a mutual daring of performing a mode of reduction that has no counterpart whatsoever in Husserl's writings. I shall consider this possibility in due course.

If Levinas rejects reduction yet retains intentional analysis, his younger contemporary Michel Henry (1922–2002) almost completely overturns what Husserl means by "phenomenology" while remaining, for all intents and purposes, within its fold. It is a crucial instance of just how far one can deviate from Husserl and still abide within his ambit. In his main work, *The Essence of Manifestation* (1963), Henry criticizes both Husserl and Heidegger, both of whom value transcendence. For Husserl, everything outside consciousness is transcendent, and even some things within it are as well (e.g., a memory of a past event); and we bring these things to the immanence of transcendental consciousness by reduction. And for Heidegger, Dasein seeks to transcend the circumstances in which it finds itself. This is not an accidental situation, as though one might leave consciousness from time to time and venture into the outside world. Not at all: Heidegger rejects the very heritage of Cartesianism, which Husserl modifies, embraces, and extends. Instead, he maintains that Dasein's very being *is* an act of transcendence. Dasein is being-in-the-world (*In-der-Welt-sein*). In Henry's view, neither Husserl nor Heidegger gives a satisfactory account of the immanence of life, and it is precisely life that should be the subject of phenomenology, he believes. Accordingly, Henry is far less interested in the phenomenon that appears than in its property to manifest itself according to its possible modes of givenness. This property is what Husserl called "phenomenality." Intentionality has masked phenomenality, Henry thinks, and removing this mask is essential for us to appreciate the self-appearing of life. Accordingly, he develops a nonintentional phenomenology.

Already, then, we can see Henry taking several decisive steps away from Husserl: his eye is on phenomenality, not the phenomenon; he is skeptical about the need for intentionality, which he regards as a metaphysics of representation; and his chief concern is not with the transcendence of the world but with the pure immanence of life. Henry's critique of the founding fathers of

---

[34] See Levinas, *Autrement que savoir*, avec des études de Guy Pettidemange and Jacques Rolland (Paris: Osiris, 1988), 74.

phenomenology reaches all the way back to the modern understanding of Descartes. In this tradition, "I think" has come to mean "I represent," and indeed we have forgotten what Descartes knew well, that we feel our seeing (*sentimus nos videre*): It is self-givenness that is original and it occurs not by way of representation but in auto-affection.[35] In short, modern philosophy has largely been a matter of "ontological monism," the view that being is inherently alienated, exterior to consciousness, which can be overcome only by representing being to consciousness by way of concepts. Only rarely – above all with Meister Eckhart (1260–c. 1328), Descartes, Fichte, Maine de Biran (1776–1824), Arthur Schopenhauer (1788–1860), and Karl Marx (1818–83) – has the western philosophical tradition glimpsed the primacy of immanent life, although it can also be seen far earlier in the West, most notably in the Gospel of John.[36] It is the enduring prejudice of ontological monism, Henry thinks, that has led to the devaluing of immanence. In fact, he goes a step further, arguing that transcendence rests upon immanence. Manifestation is first of all an affectively based self-giving of subjectivity to itself, and only derivatively a disclosure of something in the world. At heart our subjectivity remains invisible, dark, solitary, forever caught between suffering, on the one hand, and joy, on the other. These two are the most basic instances of phenomenality, and one of Henry's main claims is that they phenomenalize themselves.

If we ask ourselves what, apart from his vocabulary, keeps Henry within the fold of phenomenology, we will most likely have to answer: his concern with the question "How?" As he says, "If the question of phenomenology, which alone can define itself, is the question of the givenness not of objects but of their how, then only the theme of radical immanence as transcendental affectivity will allow it to complete its agenda."[37] Kierkegaard would have valued this stress on the "how," although without appreciating the exact nuance that the adverb has for Henry, Heidegger, or Husserl. As Kierkegaard says, "spiritually understood the road is: *how* it is walked": it's not a matter of space and time but of one's manner of being.[38] He would also have approved Henry's forceful stress on the subjective pole of human existence, while noting differences in their understandings of subjectivity, and would have been drawn to his emphasis on life (and indeed love), for he thought that life must be lived forwards, not backwards; the "how" offers a constant challenge to be what one commends,

---

[35] Michel Henry, *The Genealogy of Psychoanalysis*, trans. Douglas Brick (Stanford, CA: Stanford University Press, 1993), 70, and *Material Phenomenology*, trans. Scott Davidson (New York: Fordham University Press, 2008), 81.

[36] See Henry, *Words of Christ*, trans. Christina Gschwandtner, foreword Jean-Yves Lacoste, intro. Karl Hefty (Grand Rapids, MI: Eerdmans, 2012).

[37] Henry, *Material Phenomenology*, 81.   [38] Kierkegaard, *UDVS*, 291.

a practice he calls "reduplication." Considering Henry, even momentarily, might have given us faith that there could be reason to number Kierkegaard among the phenomenologists, but we need a better reason than the mere flexibility of the word "phenomenology" to make the attempt worthwhile. Since Henry considers Kierkegaard in some detail, I shall be returning to him in the next section.

To give a final example of how French philosophers have extended or modified Husserl's thought, I turn to Jean-Luc Marion (b. 1946). Marion has long been attracted to extreme positions in phenomenology. He values Levinas for his insistence that the other person is an enigma and the burden that this places on the self; and he appreciates Henry for the boldness of his elevation of phenomenality over the phenomenon. He is far less influenced by that most reasonable and irenic of philosophers Paul Ricœur (1913–2005), or that most exacting reader of philosophical texts Jacques Derrida (1930–2004). Marion's own radicality stems from his devotion to the early Husserl: in particular, the five lectures given in Göttingen in 1907 and subsequently published as *The Idea of Phenomenology* (1973). It is here, even more clearly than in the fifth of the *Logical Investigations*, that we see Husserl audaciously departing from Neo-Kantian epistemology and establishing his own method, one that turns on apprehending "absolute self-givenness" with all possible clarity and rigor.[39] This is the Husserl who treasures intuition and who has not yet introduced intentionality into his vision, which happens six years later in *Ideas* 1. Early phenomenology, freed from psychologism, not yet partly driven by intentionality, and already experimenting with reduction, is where Marion grounds himself; and it is this starting point that enables him to develop his distinctive theory of the saturated phenomenon.

Many phenomena, Marion argues, are saturated in intuition. If one looks at the Kantian table of categories in *The Critique of Pure Reason*, B 106, one finds opportunities to delineate four types of saturation. Events are unforeseeable, saturated with respect to quantity; idols (e.g., paintings) dazzle us, for they saturate quality; the flesh auto-affects – we feel ourselves feeling – and is absolute, so relation is saturated; and the icon (the face of the other person) cannot be objectified because it saturates modality.[40] (One will immediately notice a bow to Henry with respect to the auto-affection of the flesh and another to Levinas with regards to the face of the other person.) In some ways, then, Marion is intensely loyal to Husserl, except that he sees the master deviating from his own early, radical insight. Where Husserl came to regard

---

[39] See Husserl, *The Idea of Phenomenology*, 6,

[40] See Jean-Luc Marion, *Being Given: Toward a Phenomenology of Givenness*, trans. Jeffrey L. Kosky (Stanford, CA: Stanford University Press, 2002), §§ 21–22.

phenomenality as a hybrid notion, shared between the phenomenon and transcendental consciousness, Marion, following Henry, regards phenomenality as belonging by right to the phenomenon.[41] Few philosophers have thought longer or harder about the reduction than Marion: In *Reduction and Givenness* (1998) he proposes a third reduction, not just to objects (Husserl) or to being (Heidegger) but to givenness itself.

More striking still, Marion develops what he calls an "erotic reduction." The Cartesian insight – "I think therefore I am" – provides certainty about my existence but at the risk of living a life of sheer emptiness. Only love provides access to being and gives me a reason to live. If I ask, "Does anyone out there love me?" any possible answer will come from another person, and in that case I relinquish my deepest inner life to that person. Erotic reduction does not lead to certainty, as Husserl had hoped would happen with transcendental reduction. Instead, it exposes a lack in myself that can be filled only by another person.[42] So we have one more phenomenologist, this time someone who keeps transcendental consciousness at arm's length, who is less interested in certainty than in the insufficiency of one's own being, and who responds to Levinas's affirmation of the other person less by way of ethics than by way of love. A philosopher of love, Marion is additionally a thinker of sacrifice and revelation, two things that would be important to us were this a longer study, for Kierkegaard is deeply involved with each of them. One might think Marion would be receptive to Kierkegaard, but the Danish thinker receives only passing attention from him.[43] Nonetheless, there is reason to bring the Frenchman and the Dane into conversation, although I will not be doing that here.

Let us return, finally, to German phenomenology, specifically to Max Scheler (1874–1928) who, interestingly enough, does not appear on Marion's horizon except as a few separated dots.[44] Scheler's contributions to the new philosophy included religious experience as well as ethics, love, and social theory. Scheler,

---

[41] See Husserl, "The Amsterdam Lectures," *Psychological and Transcendental Phenomenology and the Confrontation with Heidegger*, 247.

[42] See Marion, *The Erotic Phenomenon*, trans. Stephen E. Lewis (Chicago: University of Chicago Press, 2006).

[43] Marion mentions Kierkegaard in several of his books but the largest scattering of refences is in his *Revelation Comes from Elsewhere*, trans. Stephen E. Lewis and Stephanie Rumpza (Stanford, CA: Stanford University Press, 2024), 94, 157, 280–81, 283, 433–34 n. 33.

[44] See Marion, *On Descartes' Metaphysical Prism: The Constitution and Limits of Onto-Theology in Cartesian Thought*, trans. Jeffrey L. Kosky (Chicago: University of Chicago Press, 1999), 334 n. 54; *In the Self's Place: The Approach of Saint Augustine*, trans. Jeffrey L. Kosky (Stanford, CA: Stanford University Press, 2012), 353 n. 58, *Givenness and Revelation*, trans. Stephen E. Lewis (Oxford: Oxford University Press, 2016), 37 n. 9, and *Revelation Comes from Elsewhere*, 419 n. 21 and 426 n. 30.

too, diverged from Husserl, finding the master overly preoccupied by methodological concerns, such as ἐποχή and reduction; meanwhile, Husserl took a dim view of Scheler's penchant for eloquent philosophizing in coffee houses. What is vital in phenomenology, for Scheler, is the cast of mind it promotes, an openness to the wonder of being. Seen rightly, it is what we would now call a "spiritual exercise."[45] For Scheler, the disclosure of something being evident (*Evidenz*) has its own mode of givenness, which is quite different from what we find in rational proof. Positive revelation is not to be dismissed as above or beyond the reach of phenomenological investigation; it has an εἶδος (transl. *eidos*) of its own that cannot be transposed to something outside the experience of revelation. One can intend the divine as transcendent and so form a correlation with it; and yet the initiative is always God's. Only he can manifest himself to me, publicly or privately, and he will do so in distinct ways for the Christian, the Muslim, and the Buddhist, among others. Of course, the unique manner of divine givenness means that one's experience of revelation cannot be generalized; it is of no help to apologetics.

There is space here to bring Scheler and Kierkegaard into conversation. Like Scheler, Kierkegaard is fully committed to historical revelation, and he maintains that anyone who affirms Christianity as a positive religion cannot persuade another by his or her natural gifts of intelligence or by an achieved wisdom but only by way of an authority conferred by Christ.[46] Both philosophers also diagnose the malaise of *ressentiment* in modern life. More importantly, both take love, especially ἀγάπη (transl. *agapē*), as central to their thought, and each of them, in his own way, offers a phenomenology of it: Kierkegaard in his *Works of Love* (1847) and Scheler in "Ordo Amoris" (1916) and elsewhere.[47] One advantage of leaguing Kierkegaard with Scheler is that the latter was disinclined to think of phenomenology as so many protocols and theses but rather as a fresh way of seeing, one that must be lovingly cultivated in the philosopher. Scheler had no time for what he saw as the impersonal element in Husserl's thought, consciousness as abstracted from the historical individual. He thought, instead, that human beings are perpetually striving to realize their vital energies. Only if we can harness these energies and rein them in from time to time can we gain true intuitions about the world. The position is closer in inspiration to Buddhism than to Christianity, and this needs to be kept in mind before associating Scheler too closely with Kierkegaard. (It is worth recalling that, late in life, Husserl

---

[45] See Pierre Hadot, *Philosophy as a Way of Life: Spiritual Exercises from Socrates to Foucault*, ed. Arnold Davidson (Hoboken, NJ: Wiley-Blackwell, 1995), ch. 3.

[46] See Kierkegaard, "On the Difference between a Genius and an Apostle," *WA*, 95.

[47] See, in particular, Michael Strawser, *Kierkegaard and the Philosophy of Love* (Lanham, MD: Lexington Books, 2017).

recognized that Buddhist meditation had kinship with phenomenological contemplation.)[48] Not all that Scheler wrote is phenomenology, even loosely regarded, and not all of his phenomenology can serve to bring Kierkegaard into focus as even a proto-phenomenologist. Even if we think that both philosophers propose phenomenologies of love, they do not thereby converge in all that they do.

Thinking of Marion and Scheler in the context of the conjunction "Kierkegaard and phenomenology" raises an important question: Does Kierkegaard *see* phenomenologically, even if he does not use a method we can associate with the philosophical school? And, thinking of Heidegger, we might pose another question: Does Kierkegaard see at an appropriate level for us usefully to class him as a (proto-) phenomenologist? In particular, does he discern a "how" of givenness and not just a "how" of reduplication? After all, there are many people who can pungently describe the world about them: a novelist such as Joseph Conrad (1857–1924), a poet such as Elizabeth Bishop (1911–79), and a psychoanalyst such as Sigmund Freud (1856–1939). We might demur to call them phenomenologists, however, even though Husserl was deeply interested in psychology and understood early on that poetry and phenomenology share a certain kinship.[49] Both describe an εἶδος, although where the poet describes lyrically and remains at the level of his or her psychology the philosopher describes phenomenologically in order to establish a ground for epistemic judgments.

Both questions are a little hazy, however. We can clarify them by drawing two distinctions. First, we might separate the context of discovery from the context of justification.[50] It may be that Kierkegaard sees phenomenologically but, unlike Scheler or Marion, does not present a theory, or even a bare sketch of one, that we can plausibly call phenomenological. And second, we can distinguish a historical interpretation of Kierkegaard as phenomenologist from an applicative interpretation of the same.[51] It is one thing to say that Kierkegaard is a phenomenologist as other historical figures are and another to apply his writings to the concerns of a later time, either on occasion or in general. It is sensible, it seems, to adopt a minimalist view of our theme and say that, at best,

---

[48] Husserl, "On the Teachings of Gotama Buddha," in Fred J. Hanna, "Husserl on the Teachings of the Buddha," *Humanist Psychologist*, 23 (1995), 367–68.

[49] Husserl, "Husserl an von Hofmannsthal (12.1.1907)," in *Briefwechsel*, vol. 7, 135.

[50] See Hans Reichenbach, *Experience and Prediction: An Analysis of the Foundations and the Structure of Knowledge* (Chicago: University of Chicago Press, 1938), 6–7.

[51] See Herman Philipse, *Heidegger's Philosophy of Being: A Critical Interpretation* (Princeton, NJ: Princeton University Press, 1998), 50. Also relevant here is Jacques Derrida's distinction between "belonging to" and "participating in." See his "The Law of Genre," trans. Avital Ronell, *Parages*, ed. John P. Leavey, trans. Tom Conley et al. (Stanford, CA: Stanford University Press, 2010).

Kierkegaard might be a phenomenologist in terms of the context of discovery, not the context of justification, and that we might attribute the adjective "phenomenological" to his writings, although not always, or even always with the same assurance, but not make historical claims for Kierkegaard as a phenomenologist. This situation might well be different if the conjunction we were asked to consider were "Kierkegaard and Existentialism." Then we may well find ourselves saying that historically the Dane has a sufficiently close family resemblance with other writers known as existentialist (Gabriel Marcel [1889–1973], Simone de Beauvoir [1908–86], and Sartre, among others) to make it reasonable to justify him as a plausible forerunner of the movement.[52] But even this judgment is not without caveats: We might still wish to insist on discovery, not justification. Historical movements in philosophy and theology are at best fuzzy sets. If our survey of phenomenologists has taught us anything, it will be that all its practitioners keep the question "How?" before them. If Kierkegaard does that, we have at least a thread that we can follow.

2 Kierkegaard among the Phenomenologists

As we have seen, Heidegger introduced Kierkegaard into the world of phenomenology in *Being and Time*. It is a brief introduction, by way of Vigilius Haufniensis's *The Concept of Anxiety* (Dan. *Angest*, Fr. *angoisse*, Ger. *Angst*) (1844) and a gesture towards the edifying writings, from which, he says, "there is more to be learned philosophically … than from his theoretical ones" (with the exception of the treatise on anxiety).[53] It was also a less than fulsome introduction, for while Heidegger underlines Kierkegaard's value he diminishes his achievement. He focuses on the Dane's analysis of "the moment of vision" (*Augenblik*), namely the blink of an eye when one genuinely sees past one's everyday existence, with its consoling or irritating rhythms, and into one's real situation in life, in which the future, including divine judgment, is continually pressing on one.

Kierkegaard's account of this phenomenon is adequate, Heidegger says, with respect to its *existentiell* or ontic character, although unsatisfactory at the existential or ontological level. Why is it inadequate? Because it is motivated by an uncritical, reactive emphasis on subjectivity, understood both psychologically

---

[52] See Noreen Khawaja, *The Religion of Existence: Asceticism in Philosophy from Kierkegaard to Sartre* (Chicago: University of Chicago Press, 2016).

[53] Heidegger, *Being and Time*, Div. 2, § 45, n. vi. Heidegger does not note that *The Concept of Anxiety* is a pseudonymous work. Also see Heidegger, *Ponderings XII–XV: Black Notebooks 1939–1941*, trans. Richard Rojcewicz (Bloomington: Indiana University Press, 2017), 170. Gerhard Thonhauser suggests that the "edifying works" may well be *The Sickness unto Death* and *Practice in Christianity*. See his essay " Martin Heidegger Reads Søren Kierkegaard – or What Did He Actually Read?," *Kierkegaard Studies Yearbook* (2016), no. 1, 290.

and theologically, and restricted to a traditional dynamic of time and eternity (presumably understood as uncreated life rather than everlasting life). That dynamic goes back in different ways to Hegel, Augustine, and Aristotle, all three of whom failed, in Heidegger's judgment, to think sufficiently deeply about our temporal existence.[54] Heidegger regards Dasein's temporality as the unity of three dimensions: the present, the past, and the future. We *are* these ecstases, he thinks, and we are no more than that. There is no eternal soul that we carry around inside us. (In 1930 he will archly declare, "Man is not the image of a god conceived in the sense of the absolutely bourgeois, but this latter god is the ungenuine creation of man.")[55] Chronological time, one "now" after another, merely derives from our primordial experience of mortal life. If we think of time as a series of "nows," we shall be living inauthentically. We need to think in an ontological-phenomenological manner about ourselves.

A moment of vision is a sudden flash of active insight. Existentially, it is an ecstasis, Heidegger says, a disclosure of a situation that comes into presence before us and to which we are given over. In his words, it is "the resolute rapture with which Dasein is carried away to whatever possibilities and circumstances are encountered in the Situation as possible objects of concern, but a rapture which is *held* in resoluteness."[56] Dasein is authentic when it takes charge of how it will be and so resists the pull to be what others, "the they," tell it to be. When we begin to live according to pre-given models presented to us in the media, in popular culture, or even by our friends, neighbors and employers, we cover up our being. We become inauthentic, ceasing to be the very care (*Sorge*) that we are, *viz.* living ahead of ourselves in anxiety about the future. Dasein must not become rigid in its resoluteness, however; it must hold itself open and must entertain "the possibility of *taking it back*."[57]

In thinking about the moment of vision, Heidegger looks over his shoulder to Husserl's *Logical Investigations* where, in the discussion of solitary life, "the acts in question are themselves experienced by us at that very moment [*Augenblik*]."[58] (Extending Husserl's thoughts on the subject, Fink noted that when performing reduction one's entire view of reality changes suddenly, in the blink of an eye; one experiences an "awful tremor.")[59] In addition, Heidegger

---

[54] Yet see Hegel's quite different remarks on the relation of eternity and time in his *Philosophy of Nature*, ed. Michael John Petry, 3 vols. (London: George Allen and Unwin, 1970), vol. 1, 207.

[55] Heidegger, *The Essence of Human Freedom: An Introduction to Philosophy*, trans. Ted Sadler (London: Continuum, 2002), 94.

[56] Heidegger, *Being and Time*, H. 338.   [57] Heidegger, *Being and Time*, H. 355.

[58] Husserl, *Logical Investigations*, vol. 1, 280.

[59] Fink, *Phänomenologische Werkstatt. Teilband 1: Die Doktorarbeit und erste Assistenzjahre bei Husserl*, ed. Ronald Bruzina (Freiburg: Verlag Karl Alber, 2006), 81. Also see 168. The comment on the awful tremor of reduction is to be found in *Sixth Cartesian Meditation*, 144. More generally, see William McNeill, *The Glance of the Eye: Heidegger, Aristotle, and the Ends*

would have recognized that Husserl's lectures on internal time consciousness, a version of which he sent to press in 1928, were a partial breakthrough, overcoming Aristotle's account of linear time in the *Physics* and Hegel's theory of time in the *Philosophy of Nature*.[60] For Husserl, clock-time is bracketed so that we can discern how internal time is constituted in and through consciousness; far from being one "now" after another, we experience time by way of a present marked by protentions and retentions. Nonetheless, Heidegger rejected Husserl's emphasis on consciousness and his bracketing of existence in order to manifest essence; and his mature position was quite different from his mentor's: "*The essence of Dasein lies in its existence*," he writes.[61] Nor is Heidegger beholden to Husserl's idea of philosophy as a rigorous science, and he freely appropriates another tradition, drawing from Protestant theology, chiefly Kierkegaard and Luther, as well as from the Apostle Paul. The idea of a decisive moment goes back to the word καιρός (transl. *kairos*), used often in the New Testament to denote the fitting time to act. (See, for example, Mark 12:2, Matt. 16:3, and Luke 20:10.) But let us stay just with Kierkegaard and see more exactly why Heidegger finds his treatment of anxiety insufficiently phenomenological.

In Johannes Climacus's *Concluding Unscientific Postscript* (1846) we read, "to become what one is" is "so very difficult, indeed, the most difficult of all, because every human being has a strong natural desire and drive to become something else and more."[62] Such is the heart of Kierkegaard's notion of authenticity. Johannes Climacus is not the most fully Christian of Kierkegaard's characters; even so, he thinks that the notion of authenticity is thoroughly imbricated in Christianity, which "wants the subject to be infinitely concerned about himself."[63] For Kierkegaard, in the blink of an eye one can see through time to eternity and see one's existence absolutely at stake.[64] In *The Concept of Anxiety*, we read, "Man, then, is a synthesis of psyche and body, but he is also a *synthesis of the temporal and the eternal*." He continues by pondering the relation of time and eternity. Time is "an infinite succession, it most likely is also defined as the present, the past, and the future," a distinction that Kierkegaard thinks can appear only "through the relation of time to eternity." Actually, it is in the moment that "time and eternity" touch each other and so not just a moment like any other. (Since they merely touch,

---

of Theory (Albany: State University of New York Press, 1999), 114–23, and Koral Ward, *Augenblik: The Concept of the "Decisive Moment" in Nineteenth- and Twentieth-Century Western Philosophy* (Aldershot: Ashgate, 2008).

[60] See Aristotle, *Physics*, 4.10–14, and Hegel, *Philosophy of Nature*, vol. 1, section 1, ch. 1 B. The bulk of the work on Husserl's lectures was actually done by Edith Stein.

[61] Heidegger, *Being and Time*, H. 42.   [62] Kierkegaard, *CUP*, vol. 1, 130.

[63] Kierkegaard, *CUP*, vol. 1, 130.   [64] See Kierkegaard, *NB* 17: 43

a nontheoretical sense, there can be no theoretical confirmation of the conjunction.) To be sure, a blink of the eye is "a designation of time, but mark well, of time in the fateful conflict when it is touched by eternity."[65] It is the moment when one might leap from this shore to the other one.[66] As Kierkegaard reminds us, Plato talks about flashes of insight that come upon one suddenly (ἐξαίφνης, transl. *exaiphnes*) and mark significant changes. Examples are found in the *Republic* 516e 3–4, *Parmenides* 156d1–e7, and the *Seventh Letter* 341c8–d1. The sudden moment for Plato is out of time (*Parmenides* 132d), while for Kierkegaard it's not "an atom of time but an atom of eternity."[67]

When we read Kierkegaard on the moment of vision, and more generally on authenticity, it is tempting to claim that Heidegger de-theologizes the Dane's Christian insights.[68] (One might think the same with regard to his uses of Luther, Augustine, and Paul.) But one must be careful in making such a judgment. It is not that Heidegger translates theism into atheism but, rather, that, in reading Kierkegaard, he seeks a more radical position, "outside of Christianity, outside of theology, and outside of metaphysics."[69] If we use the word "de-theologize" we must be aware that the "de-" means "away from" and "removal," as well as "reversal." Yet the negative movement belies a positive one: a resetting of the question of being. Dasein is not a "self" or "subject" without God; it is a structure of being anterior to any encounter with God, although one that would come into conflict with any articulated mode of Christianity.[70] All this is said in the awareness that Heidegger's relationship to Kierkegaard varies over the course of his writing life. In 1920 he hails the Dane's "methodological rigor," which had "rarely been achieved in philosophy or theology."[71] In the 1930s he says of his own central concept, "existence," that in its various iterations it belongs to the history of metaphysics. One of these iterations is "Existence in Kierkegaard's sense, only without the essential relation to Christian faith."[72] Philosophically considered, then, Kierkegaard's view of human existence is metaphysical (as Heidegger comes to think of his

---

[65] Kierkegaard, *CA*, 87.

[66] The idea of "the leap" is Kierkegaard's. It is worth noting, however, that Heidegger develops the notion in his *The Principle of Reason*, trans. Reginald Lilly (Bloomington: Indiana University Press, 1991).

[67] Kierkegaard, *CA*, 85–88.   [68] See Philipse, *Heidegger's Philosophy of Being*, 259.

[69] Heidegger, *Ponderings, XII–XV,* 169.

[70] See Heidegger's 1928 letter to Julius Stenzel as quoted by Hugo Ott, *Martin Heidegger: A Political Life*, trans. Allan Blunden (London: HarperCollins, 1993), 163.

[71] Heidegger, "Comments on Karl Jaspers's *Psychology of Worldviews*," trans. John van Buren, *Supplements: From the Earliest Essays to "Being and Time" and Beyond*, ed. John van Buren (Albany: State University of New York Press, 2002), 101.

[72] Heidegger, "Sketches for a History of Being as Metaphysics," *The End of Philosophy*, trans. Joan Stambaugh (Chicago: University of Chicago Press, 1973), 70.

own sense of Dasein's temporal ecstases). Later still, he will make the point to Jean Beaufret in 1964 that Kierkegaard is not so much a philosopher as a thinker, which for him at the time was a positive valuation.[73]

In *Being and Time*, his program of transforming the theology of the subject in Kierkegaard's writings does not come from an impulse stemming from Hegelian or Husserlian phenomenology but as a consequence of his own thinking about historicality in *Being and Time*, § 74, where we learn that "the Being of this entity [*Dasein*] is constituted by historicality" and that the concrete working out of temporality is resolute attention to the historical moment.[74] "The resoluteness in which Dasein comes back to itself, discloses current factical possibilities of authentic existing," he writes, "and discloses them *in terms of the heritage* which that resoluteness, as thrown, *takes over*."[75] Historical constitution excludes eternity, it seems, which for him remains a metaphysical category. In 1933, still in the wake of *Being and Time* and the seminars of 1927, Dasein can take over the factical possibilities, embedded in Germany's past, and now revived for the present and future, represented not by any religious writer but by the rise of the National Socialist Party. In April 1933 Heidegger became rector of the University of Freiburg and joined the Party ten days later.

Kierkegaard urges us, through certain of his pseudonyms (and eventually in his own name), to become radically Christian in order to stand apart from "the world" in Paul's sense (see, e.g., 1 Cor. 2:12) and thus to enter the Kingdom of God. Heidegger meanwhile is committed unconditionally to "the world" in his sense of the word, namely "environment" – Dasein *is* nothing more than being-in-the-world – and can only urge us to be resolute in our encounter with what is to come, or, as we have seen, to withdraw our resolution, if need be. Christians such as Karl Barth (1886–1968), Dietrich Bonhoeffer (1906–45), and Konrad von Preysing (1880–1950) had grounds for resisting the National Socialists: They glimpsed what Erich Przywara (1889–1972) nicely calls "the incidence of eternity."[76] But Heidegger had written himself into a corner where he had no

---

[73] In his written contribution to the UNESCO conference in April 1964, later edited by René Maheu and published as *Kierkegaard vivant* (Paris: Gallimard, 1966), Heidegger does not mention the Danish thinker. Jean Beaufret indicates why in his introduction to Heidegger's talk "The End of Philosophy and the Task of Thinking," which may be found in his *On Time and Being*, trans. Joan Stambaugh (New York: Harper and Row, 1972). Yet see Heidegger's earlier view in his *Ponderings, II–VI: Black Notebooks 1931–1938*, trans. Richard Rojcewicz (Bloomington: Indiana University Press, 2016), § 183. Finally, for a deflation of whether Kierkegaard always writes either philosophy or theology, see Jean-Yves Lacoste, "The Missing Frontier: Philosophy and Theology in the *Philosophical Fragments*," *The Appearing of God*, trans. Oliver O'Donovan (Oxford: Oxford University Press, 2018), 1–18.

[74] Heidegger, *Being and Time*, H. 382.   [75] Heidegger, *Being and Time*, H. 383.

[76] Erich Przywara, *Analogia Entis: Metaphysics: Original Structure and Universal Rhythm*, trans. John R. Betz and David Bentley Hart (Grand Rapids, MI: Eerdmans, 2014), 242.

such foundation available to him. His only recourse would have been taking back his resolution, which he did not do, at least not until April 1934 when he resigned from the rectorate, and, more likely, not until he left the Nazi Party in 1945, or even later, if indeed ever. If we step back from the rhetoric of *Being and Time* just a little, it is perhaps difficult to see that the existential thinking about time in Heidegger's construal of Dasein is any more phenomenologically grounded than Kierkegaard's Christian reflections on being able to glimpse eternity. He remains oriented by the claim that philosophy is ontological whereas theology is merely ontic and fails to see that phenomenology is a current in theology as well as in philosophy.[77] But then we have yet to see more surely what the Dane means by "eternity."

Even before we get that far, we might pose a question: Why would a fundamental view of Dasein's threefold ecstasies disclose more about being human than a commitment to Christian faith? The reason, for Heidegger, would turn on Kierkegaard's remaining within a rigid schema of time as *nunc* after *nunc* and eternity as *nunc stans* and, within that, of regarding eternity by way of personal salvation, thereby adopting a metaphysics of subjectivity. For Heidegger, none of this can be phenomenological because it is beholden to a pre-given division of the natural and spiritual orders (i.e., natural reason and divine faith), a division that misses, as Eberhard Jüngel points out, "the true dignity of time."[78] Of course, we may wonder in turn if Heidegger's insistence that we are bodily beings is itself not a reductive view of human being without phenomenological support. Could it not be argued, as Conrad-Martius and Stein have both done against Heidegger, that the "I" has relations with its body and soul?[79] If so, there is more space for a thinking of the human orientation to eternity as well as to time. In any case, we must be wary of accepting Heidegger's thought of eternity wholly in philosophical or neo-scholastic terms as strongly contrasting in one way or another with time and be especially wary of thinking of Kierkegaard as inheriting such an idea from Hegel.[80] The heritage comes to us primarily from

---

[77] Heidegger becomes more open to the independence of theology from philosophy in his 1970 preface to "Phenomenology and Theology." See *Pathmarks*, ed. William McNeill (Cambridge: Cambridge University Press, 1998), 39.

[78] Eberhard Jüngel, *God as the Mystery of the World: On the Foundation of the Theology of the Crucified One in the Dispute between Theism and Atheism*, trans. Darrell L. Guder (Grand Rapids, MI: William B. Eerdmans Pub. Co., 1983), 213. Jüngel considers Kierkegaard's notion of possibility as overcoming the *nunc stans*, and this occurs by thinking "God in unity with perishability," 214.

[79] See Heidegger, *Nietzsche*, 4 vols., vol. 1: *The Will to Power as Art*, trans. David Farrell Kresll (San Francisco, CA: Harper and Row, 1979), 99, Conrad-Martius, *Bios und Psyche* (Hamburg: Classen and Goverts, 1949), and Stein, "Martin Heidegger's Existential Philosophy," trans. Mette Lebech, *Maynooth Philosophical Papers*, vol. 4 (2007), 55–98.

[80] H. S. Harris points out that Hegel argues that this world is actually "a training-ground" for the "other" eternal one. See his *Hegel's Ladder*, 2 vols, vol. 1: *The Pilgrimage of Reason* (Indianapolis: Hackett, 1997), 252–53.

Boethius's *The Consolation of Philosophy* (c. 524) where we learn that eternity is "the complete, simultaneous and perfect possession of everlasting life."[81] This view became important in the Middle Ages (in particular, for Anselm [d. 1109] and Abelard [1079–1142]) in discussions of future contingents and divine fore-knowledge of earthly events.

For later Christians, however, including Kierkegaard, eternity is thought otherwise. Where Heidegger figures time and eternity by way of contrast (and thus renders it metaphysical), one might point out that Christianity understands contrast to exist only in time and that eternity is irreducible to its terms. Eternity does not contrast with time; it can therefore freely enter it.[82] We might say that eternity is fundamentally the gift of participating in divine love, the gift of a new quality of life, a rebirth, though one that is gained only by self-sacrifice on our part and by Grace on God's part.[83] Life, here, is ζωή (transl. *zoē*), which in the New Testament is often used to indicate eternal life, as when Jesus is asked, "what good deed must I do, to have eternal life?" (τί ἀγαθὸν ποιήσω ἵνα σχῶ ζωὴν αἰώνιον) (Matt. 19:16). This is not life in the sense of βίος (transl. *bios*), biological life. Eternal life can occur here and now as well as continuing in another mode after death. It is one of the manifestations of what Christ calls the Kingdom. By contrast, Heidegger's "originary temporalizing" has no related notion of eternity at all: He would reject Boethius's view and would not accept the idea of eternity as a nonbiological quality of life. In some ways, his notion of being resolute is a substitute for it. For Heidegger, as early as the projected second part of *Being and Time*, not only is Dasein finite but also he is clear that being (or, as he comes to say, "beyng") is finite as well: It "illuminates itself as the most finite and richest."[84]

In very broad outlines, the idea that being is finite goes back to the second fragment of the poem of Parmenides (d. 460 BC): If being is to be intelligible, as he thought, then it must be finite, and "infinite being" would therefore be a contradiction in terms. Only with Gregory of Nyssa (c. 335–c. 394) and, later, Aquinas, for whom the deity is its own essence, is God regarded as metaphysically infinite.[85] Heidegger takes his cues from Friedrich Nietzsche (1844–1900), rather than Aquinas, and consequently comes to maintain in the 1930s that "Nihilism is the history of being itself, through which the death of the

---

[81] Boethius, *The Consolation of Philosophy*, trans. V. E. Watts (London: Penguin, 1969), 5.6. Also see Aquinas, *Summa theologiæ*, 1a q. 10 art. 4 *resp.*

[82] See Robert Sokolowski, *The God of Faith and Reason: Foundations of Christian Theology* (Washington, DC: Catholic University of America Press, 1982), esp. ch. 2.

[83] See Kierkegaard, *KJN* 4: 112, 11: 105, 27: 39.

[84] Heidegger, *Contributions to Philosophy (of the Event)*, trans. Richard Rojcewicz and Daniella Vallega-Neu (Bloomington: Indiana University Press, 2012), § 123.

[85] See Aquinas, *Summa theologiæ*, 1a q. 7 art. 1 *resp.*

Christian God comes slowly but inexorably to light."[86] (One cannot avoid seeing an eerie double here, for Heidegger's thesis "The essence of Dasein lies in its existence" construes Dasein as a mortal god.) Is there any coercive reason to justify phenomenology as necessarily favoring a finitude leagued to thought? Stein points out that everywhere Heidegger erects barriers for Dasein to view the eternal and that his picture of Dasein is at heart one of unredeemed being. More pointedly, she shows that his view of Dasein's finitude is problematic. On the one hand, because Heidegger figures finitude by reference to the end of life and not by an appeal to infinitude, he considers the meaning of Dasein to be given in death, while, on the other hand, he says that he makes no decision about the hope for life beyond death.[87] Yet it may well be possible for Dasein to have another mode of being after death. Can we go any further in this line of inquiry?

We can recall that Christians profess to live in and through the Word of God and believe that phenomenality is a property of Christ, even if this modern vocabulary is seldom used outside academic theology. We read of the incarnation, "The true light that enlightens every man was coming into the world" (John 1: 9). Christianity is not simply a matter of living temporality as such, not even in abiding in the "how" of the gospel proclamation and anticipating the end times, as Heidegger suggested.[88] (One must be careful not to allow John's κόσμος and Heidegger's *Welt* to converge without question.) For those with faith, "the tension of passion," it is not always an experience of anxiety (Luke 12:22, 1 Thes. 5:8–11), although it can be an experience of impatience, even suffering, and a demand for decision sooner rather than later.[89] It is certainly not a matter of dying as one's mode of being. Rather, it is living as being-attracted-to-God, which one can sometimes glimpse in the death of others, and which gives one a far broader horizon than living according to one's historical horizons, whatever they may be.[90] More, it is living in hope of a more complete conforming of one's being to Christ. If that can be achieved through Grace one is never alone, not even in death, despite what Heidegger says on death as nonrelational in *Being and Time* ¶ 53. It is a hope that can be understood by grasping the "how" of living in "morning knowledge."

---

[86] Heidegger, *Nietzsche*, vol. 4: *Nihilism*, trans. Frank A. Capuzzi, ed. David Farrell Krell (San Francisco, CA: Harper and Row, 1982), 4. More generally, on Heidegger's development of an eschatology without an eschaton, see Judith Wolfe, *Heidegger's Eschatology: Theological Horizons in Martin Heidegger's Early Work* (Oxford: Oxford University Press, 2013), esp. ch. 6, and *Heidegger and Theology* (London: Bloomsbury, 2014), 3 and *passim*.

[87] See Stein, "Martin Heidegger's Existential Philosophy," 82, 81, 75.

[88] See Heidegger, *The Phenomenology of Religious Life*, trans. Matthias Fritsch and Jennifer Anna Gosetti-Ferencei (Bloomington: Indiana University Press, 2004), part 2.

[89] See Kierkegaard, *NB* 27: 39, *NB* 26: 82 and *NB* 31: 2.   [90] Kierkegaard, *NB* 20: 70.

The idea of morning knowledge goes back to Augustine's *Literal Commentary on Genesis* (401–15) and indicates an awareness of divine love suffusing creation, not just the knowledge of things as they are, which is "evening knowledge."[91] To live in the "how" of morning knowledge is to conform oneself to Christ, in the love that he freely gives, and that he showed in his life, suffering, and death. One might make a second riposte to Heidegger. For one may well suggest that the moment of vision, as Kierkegaard figures it, can lead us back to God. It is not a reduction in Husserl's sense, a passage to transcendental life, but a movement back to transcendent Life. It is a *reductio in mysterium*, as Przywara might have said (with Edith Stein nodding in agreement while slightly changing the expression to *reductio ad mysterium*), and so it is phenomenological in quite another way than the one that Heidegger proposed.[92] It absorbs us with the mystery of God rather than the mystery of being.

It is the French, more than the Germans, who have hailed Kierkegaard as a forerunner of phenomenology or who have attributed phenomenological insight to him. Even Karl Jaspers, who valued Kierkegaard, thought his pseudonymous writings prevented him from engaging in the strict analysis of states of consciousness which makes one a phenomenologist.[93] As early as 1938, Jean Wahl (1888–1974) championed the Danish thinker in his *Études kierkegaardiennes* not as a philosophical oddity, as he had been regarded before then, but as a coherent thinker of existence and human subjectivity, and was largely responsible for Kierkegaard being welcomed as a forerunner of existentialism. (Early on, in December 1941, Maurice Blanchot echoes Wahl in speaking of the Dane's motivating idea as "existence itself.")[94] At an angle to Wahl's project, we find Maurice Merleau-Ponty (1908–61) writing, at the very start of his *Phenomenology of Perception* (1945), that the coming of phenomenology "has been long on the way, and its adherents have discovered it in every quarter,

---

[91] See Augustine, "Literal Commentary on Genesis," *On Genesis*, trans. Edmund Hill, ed. John E. Rotelle, The Works of Saint Augustine, 1/13 (Hyde Park, NY: New City Press, 2002), book 4, and Thomas Aquinas, *Commentary on the Gospel of John*, 2 vols., trans. Fabian R. Larcher, ed. Aquinas Institute (Green Bay, WI: Aquinas Institute, 2013), § 118, and *Summa theologiæ*, 1a q. 58 art. 6, *resp.*

[92] Przywara acknowledges the inspiration of Husserl, Heidegger, Scheler, and Stein in his preface to the 1932 edition of the book *Analogia Entis*, xxi. See Edith Stein, *Finite and Eternal Being*, trans. Kurt F. Reinhardt (Washington, DC: ICS Publications, 2002), 25.

[93] See Karl Jaspers, *Reason and Existenz: Five Lectures*, trans. William Earle (New York: Noonday Press, 1957). Also see *The Great Philosophers*, vol. 4: *Descartes, Pascal, Lessing, Kierkegaard, Nietzsche, Marx, Weber, Einstein*, ed. Michael Ermarth, trans. Edith Ehrlich, 4 vols. (New York: Houghton Mifflin Harcourt, 1995).

[94] Maurice Blanchot, "Kierkegaard's *Journals*," *Faux Pas*, trans. Charlotte Mandell (Stanford, CA: Stanford University Press, 2001), 17.

certainly in Hegel and Kierkegaard, but equally in Marx, Nietzsche and Freud."[95] It is one of the strongest historical claims for Kierkegaard as phenomenologist on record.

Not all French philosophers have sought to align themselves even loosely with the Dane, however. Levinas, in particular, sometimes sets himself in opposition to him on important points. In an interview with François Poirié conducted in 1986 he is asked about his views on anguish as they appear in *Existence and Existents* (1947). He responds: "It is not the anguish of nothing, it is the horror of the *there is*, of existence. It is not the fear of death; it is the 'too much' of oneself." Then he distinguishes himself in no uncertain terms from the two major figures in the literature on *Angst*: "It's true, since Heidegger and even since Kierkegaard, anguish is analyzed as the emotion of not being, as the anguish before [the] nothing, whereas the horror of the *there is* is close to disgust for oneself, close to the wariness of oneself."[96] (This passing evocation of Kierkegaard misses the important point that anxiety, for him, is a tension of the finite and the infinite, an exposure to freedom and a fear of the responsibility that this entails.) Even more sharply, Levinas observes in *Totality and Infinity* (1961) primarily with respect to Hegel: "It is not I who resist the system, as Kierkegaard thought; it is the other."[97] This last laconic remark is expanded in a considered response to the UNESCO conference "Kierkegaard vivant," held in Paris in April 1964 at which a number of European philosophers, including Heidegger and Jaspers, Gabriel Marcel and Sartre, addressed what is living and dead in the thought of the Dane.[98] Levinas takes issue with Kierkegaard on two main points: (1) his rehabilitation of subjectivity and (2) his violence with respect to ethics. Let us look at these one at a time.

First, Levinas acknowledges the "incomparable strength" with which Kierkegaard revived subjectivity in the wake of Hegelianism, especially as it affected the Danish academy, where the individual human subject had been largely strangled by the relentless growth of the kudzu vine of the dialectic. The upshot of this vitality, though, is "an exhibitionistic, immodest subjectivity," which the intellectual currents of the day have sought to dampen. He is thinking of the rebirth of Hegel studies, centered on Jean Hyppolite's influential *Genesis and Structure of Hegel's "Phenomenology of Spirit"* (1947) and *Logic and Existence* (1952). Other enthusiasms sre likewise in play: excitement for the

---

[95] Maurice Merleau-Ponty, *Phenomenology of Perception*, trans. Colin Smith (London: Routledge and Kegan Paul, 1962), viii.

[96] Jill Robbins, ed., *Is it Righteous to Be? Interviews with Emmanuel Levinas* (Stanford, CA: Stanford University Press, 2002), 46.

[97] Levinas, *Totality and Infinity: An Essay on Exteriority*, trans. Alphono Lingis (The Hague: Martinus Nijhoff, 1979), 40.

[98] See Maheu, ed., *Kierkegaard vivant*. Heidegger's paper was read by Jean Beaufret.

later work of Heidegger (Jean Beaufret and François Fédier), ardor for the rediscovery of Marx (Lucien Goldmann and Louis Althusser), and passion for the rise of structuralism and semiotics (Claude Lévi-Strauss and Roland Barthes). In reacting so sharply to the dialectic, Levinas thinks, Kierkegaard develops a notion of subjectivity that is without form.[99] It stimulates the counter-movements I have just mentioned.

Second, Kierkegaard's violence becomes all too apparent in his drive to overcome ethics by way of a hyper-religiousness of the individual, most notably in the writings of Anti-Climacus. "The singularity of the *I* would be lost, in his view, under a rule valid for all," Levinas writes. Doubtless this is true if we are thinking of the Kantian categorical imperative or Hegel's *Sittlichkeit* (ethical life); but, Levinas suggests, the Danish thinker looked for ethics in the wrong place. The right place, it seems, is just where Levinas situates it in *Totality and Infinity*, namely in one's relation to the other person. "Ethics as consciousness of a responsibility towards others . . . far from losing you in generality, singularizes you, poses you as a unique individual, as *I*."[100] (Blanchot will judiciously point out that this "I" is never unique: "in me anyone at all is called by the other.")[101] As noted in the previous section, Climacus distinguishes persistently between Religiousness A and B, the latter being marked by a strong conviction of sinfulness which renders God wholly other. This separates him from Levinas.

Kierkegaard's most memorable case in favor of Religiousness B is Johannes de Silentio's extensive midrash on Genesis 22:1–19, the book we know as *Fear and Trembling* (1843), which looks intently at the Akedah, Abraham's binding of Isaac. For Kierkegaard, the sharp point of the story is God's call for Abraham to sacrifice his only son. To answer the call, Abraham's faith must be shown to pierce the general claim of morality on us, including that associated with Religiousness A. Abraham must hope that the single-mindedness of his faith, which leads him to break with how communities usually act, will keep him from what seems obvious to most readers: that he will grievously sin in sacrificing his son. Yet Levinas finds the climax of the biblical narrative elsewhere, in the importance of "Abraham's attentiveness to the voice that led him back to the ethical order, in forbidding him to perform a human sacrifice."[102] For Levinas, God comes to mind precisely when our perseverance in being is interrupted by the face of another person, since there we find the trace of the divine. The word

---

[99] See Levinas, "A Propos of 'Kierkegaard vivant,'" *Proper Names*, trans. Michael B. Smith (Stanford, CA: Stanford University Press, 1996), 76.

[100] Levinas, *Proper Names*, 76.

[101] Blanchot, *The Writing of the Disaster*, trans. Ann Smock (Lincoln: University of Nebraska Press, 1986), 13.

[102] Levinas, *Proper Names*, 77.

"God" signifies in "*phenomenological concreteness*," in passing from the Said to the Saying, irrespective of whether or not a deity exists and irrespective of Husserl's suspension of the question of God.[103] The relevant lived experience for Levinas is the relationship with the other person. "The kingdom of heaven is ethical," we are firmly told in *Otherwise Than Being* (1978).[104]

In another short essay on Kierkegaard, we find Levinas hinting at a more adventurous reading of the Danish thinker. In the midst of a sentence which broods on "the exaltation of pure faith" finally being a matter of "egotism," we find a second way of situating Kierkegaard. In pure faith one would have "the correlate of truth crucified" and this would be "the 'phenomenology' which no one has developed with greater rigor than Kierkegaard."[105] "Phenomenology" is set in scare quotes, since, as Levinas well knows, the orthodox way of thinking of the philosophical discipline is by way of a mental intention being cued to an intentional object, a noesis correlating with noema. In this imagined double of phenomenology, though, the noesis would be the pure faith of an Abraham that would be leagued with truth not as a neutral object but as an intentional object of faith, "truth crucified." In the essay reflecting on the conference "Kierkegaard vivant," Levinas expands on this thought:

> I think that Kierkegaard's philosophical novelty is in his idea of belief. Belief is not, for him, an imperfect knowledge of a truth that would be perfect and triumphant in itself. In his view, belief is not a small truth, a truth without certainty, a degradation of knowledge. There is, in Kierkegaard, an opposition not between faith and knowledge, in which the uncertain would be set in opposition to the certain, but between truth triumphant and truth persecuted. Persecuted truth is not simply a truth wrongly approached. Persecution and, by the same token, humility are modalities of the true. This is something completely new.[106]

One might demur about the claim of "philosophical novelty," since the rhythm of *credere deo*, *credere deum*, and *credere in deum*, which yields a fully formed faith, was established by Augustine and confirmed by Aquinas.[107] Nonetheless, one might entertain Levinas's sense that there are distinct modalities of truth, including the transcendent and the persecuted. The latter appears not as fully disclosed in all its possible profiles but only in vulnerability. It is the truth of Saying, as distinct from the truth as Said: truth as exposed rather than as already lodged in the order of being. Levinas turns to Heidegger, without naming him:

---

[103] Levinas, *Of God Who Comes to Mind*, xi.   [104] Levinas, *Otherwise Than Being*, 183
[105] Levinas, "Kierkegaard: Existence and Ethics," *Proper Names*, 70.
[106] Levinas, *Proper Names*, 77–78.
[107] See Aquinas, *Summa theologiæ*, 2a2ae q. 2 art. 2, *resp.*

"The idea of persecuted truth allows us, perhaps, to put an end to the game of disclosure, in which immanence always wins out over transcendence."[108] We may well recall Heidegger's insistence on Dasein's ecstatic finitude, however, and we may question the insistence marked by "always."

For Levinas, ethics needs a ground other than the divine commands of Torah, for our age is one in which the historical criticism has eroded confidence in the authenticity of positive revelation. His observation about biblical criticism was made almost sixty years ago. Now one would likely have a more nuanced view of the matter: Historical criticism has been challenged on several fronts, including its faith in the documentary hypothesis, and for summarily rejecting singular events (miracles, incarnation, resurrection) as unhistorical by definition. True science pauses at singularities, weighs them with care, and is not in a rush to eliminate them, since they can sometimes lead to new paradigms. Nonetheless, Levinas's point is clear: Ethics, for him, turns on the face of the other person, which is an enigma, not a phenomenon.[109] An enigma is truly exterior to consciousness. What is essential – the exposure of the other person's face, his or her vulnerability, and one's obligation to him or her – is acknowledged even before a word is actually said.

"Yet there was a message," Levinas says, while doubting the positivity of divine revelation; and he may be recalling the verse "The stranger who sojourns with you shall be to you as the native among you, and you shall love him as yourself" (Lev. 19:34). Being Jewish, Levinas cannot be expected to develop his idea based on Kierkegaard's Christian insight of pure faith having truth crucified as its correlate. His "truth crucified" is the Saying; for Christians, it is primarily Christ himself, the Word. (One can only wonder at Levinas's choice of the word "crucified.") Yet the thought can be elaborated nonetheless, for faith is a mode of intentionality, and Jesus is paradoxically the Truth that was crucified. It is entirely characteristic of Kierkegaard (here following Luther) that faith is placed in Christ in the profile of the crucified one. For this intensifies the paradox of Christianity. Kierkegaard's phenomenology, as entertained by Levinas, is at once traditional as regards Christianity and original with respect to philosophy.

In the interview with François Poirié, Levinas recalls that one year he gave seminars on Michel Henry's *The Essence of Manifestation* (1963), which he calls "an entirely exceptional book."[110] In teaching that tome, he would have

---

[108] Levinas, *Proper Names*, 78.

[109] See Levinas, "Phenomenon and Enigma," *Collected Philosophical Papers*, trans. Alphonso Lingis (The Hague: Martinus Nijhoff, 1987), 61–73.

[110] Robbins, *Is it Righteous to Be?*, 80.

read Henry's long discussion of Anti-Climacus's *The Sickness unto Death* (1849), which comes towards its end. In some ways, *The Sickness unto Death* pushes further into the themes announced and partly covered in *The Concept of Anxiety* and *Fear and Trembling*. As we have already seen, though, Anti-Climacus is a more exacting Christian than either Vigilius Haufniensis or Johannes de Silentio. He is higher up the *scala perfectionis* than any other of the pseudonymous authors that Kierkegaard brings alive. The "sickness unto death" is nothing physical, as it is in John 11:4 when Jesus hears that his friend Lazarus is ill. That sickness was allowed to occur for the glory of God in the raising of Lazarus from the dead (John 11:43–44). Anti-Climacus, however, is concerned with a spiritual sickness that leads to death, namely the sin of despair.

I have just quoted the Gospel of John, which is most likely the last of the canonical Gospels to be completed (c. 90–c. 110), and so it is opportune to point out one large difference between Henry and Levinas. Where Levinas takes the historical criticism to erode belief in God, so much so that we must look for the deity as a trace in the phenomenological concreteness of the relation with another person, Henry adopts a Kierkegaardian sense of contemporaneity. Johannes Climacus doubts that the historical knowledge that Jesus's disciples had of him was an aid to their faith: Empirical knowledge is based on accidents, and faith is a gift from God.[111] It will be underlined by Anti-Climacus that we must accept faith if we are to live with the unbearable paradox of Jesus as the crucified God.[112] One is a true contemporary of Jesus only when one has faith in him as the Christ. On that condition alone can one really perform *imitatio Christi*. Now Henry agrees wholeheartedly with Johannes Climacus and Anti-Climacus on this point. To have faith wait on historical findings for its confirmation or disconfirmation would be to remain in suspense about the truth until the end of time. "As in Kierkegaard's ironic remark," Henry says, you would have to "await the publication of the very last book on the question" and would surely die before you could get a satisfactory answer to your question as to the veracity of the Gospel. "This is because *what the answer depends upon, the truth of Christianity, has precisely no relation whatsoever to the truth that arises from the analysis of texts or their historical study.*"[113]

There is to be no passage from positive revelation to an ethics of responsibility for Henry. He will abide with the truth of Christianity. But how?

It is not the corpus of New Testament texts that can offer us access to the Truth, to that absolute Truth of which the corpus speaks. On the contrary, it is

---

[111] Kierkegaard, *PF*, section 4.   [112] Kierkegaard, *PC*, no. 1, section 4.

[113] Henry, *I am the Truth: Toward a Philosophy of Christianity*, trans. Susan Emanuel (Stanford, CA: Stanford University Press, 2003), 3.

> *Truth and Truth alone that can offer us access to itself and by the same token
> to that corpus, allowing us to understand the text in which Truth is deposited
> and to recognize it there.*[114]

Unlike Husserl and Heidegger (but like Scheler), Henry maintains that God has a distinct phenomenality, a property of self-disclosure that is entirely his own, underived from anything in the world. God phenomenalizes his own phenomenality, as Henry likes to say. That is, he makes a phenomenon of his own property of self-revelation, in and through the very person of Christ. This formulation may well be too close to Monophysitism to be of any use to orthodox Christian thought; but, for Henry, it is this event that indicates to us how we are to find the Truth to which the Gospels testify. When Jesus says, "I am the way, and the truth, and the life [ζωή]" (John 14:6), he reveals himself as Life, which he can grant to us when we follow the "how" that only he makes manifest and which the world cannot give. As we have heard Kierkegaard say once before, "spiritually understood the road is: *how* it is walked."[115] The road is "the continual transformation of the striving spirit," a matter of reduplication.[116]

We can see how thoroughly Henry follows Kierkegaard's notion of contemporality. His concern is with Truth: Christ, to be sure, but also the Truth that discloses itself in the self-revelation of Life. This revelation does not come from elsewhere; it is self-affectivity, which is wholly immanent, the immediate experience of self in the darkness of the self. If we accept this, as Henry does, the distinction between historical and attributive interpretation has no purchase. Henry would be Kierkegaard's contemporary, as well as Christ's. (There is a sense in which Henry, often to the surprise of historians of philosophy, finds his material phenomenology anticipated by John the Evangelist, Meister Eckhart, de Biran, Fichte, Schopenhauer, and Marx, and so they too become his philosophical contemporaries.) We can plainly see how utterly different his version of phenomenology is from those of Husserl, Heidegger, and Levinas. There is no reduction for Henry, and he is concerned far less with consciousness and its representations than with the self-affectivity that he takes to be anterior to all such talk. Husserl and Levinas prize intentionality; Heidegger affirms ecstases: All three thereby concern themselves with the world and what appears in it. Henry, by contrast, attends to phenomenality, which he locates not in any mode of transcendence but in the immanence of Life itself. The essence of Life is to reveal itself, not accidentally or just some of the time but always and by dint of what it is. If ethics seems to have faded from view, it should be said that, for

---

[114] Henry, *I am the Truth*, 9. [115] Kierkegaard, *UDVS*, 291.
[116] Kierkegaard, *UDVS*, 49. Also see *NB* 22: 79.

Henry, it is no more (and no less) than the putting into practice of the self-revelation of Life, namely the sharing of joy and suffering.

We are now in a position to turn to Henry's discussion of Kierkegaard's *The Sickness unto Death*. It occurs in his magisterial treatment of affectivity and the absolute in *The Essence of Manifestation*. In a note right at the start he rejects Heidegger's criticism of Kierkegaard, namely that he could analyze a phenomenon only at an *existentiell* level and not at an existential level. On the contrary, Henry writes, *The Sickness unto Death* "is not merely invested with a manifest, 'existential,' ontological meaning, but actually presupposes a conception of ontology radically different from that of the Greeks and Hegel and even from that of Heidegger himself."[117] All those thinkers have developed ontologies based on the alienation of being: a metaphysics of representation. Henry values Kierkegaard for furnishing an ontology based on the immanence of Life, which has its own possibilities. Henry agrees with Kierkegaard that despair is related to the ego, even if it seems to be connected to something in the world, namely something outside the self that makes one despair.

Let's see how Kierkegaard comes to think that despair is rooted in the self, in the immanence of Life, rather in the world about it. He does so by meditating on the motto of Cesare Borgia (1475–1507), *Aut Caesar aut nihil* ("Either Caesar or nothing"):

> For example, when the ambitious man whose slogan is "Either Caesar or nothing" does not get to be Caesar, he despairs over it. But this also means something else: precisely because he did not get to be Caesar, he now cannot bear to be himself. Consequently he does not despair because he did not get to be Caesar but despairs over himself because he did not get to be Caesar. This self, which, if it had become Caesar, would have been in seventh heaven (a state, incidentally, that is in another sense is just as despairing), this self is now utterly intolerable to him. In a deeper sense, it is not his failure to become Caesar that is intolerable, but it is this self that did not become Caesar that is intolerable; or, to put it even more accurately, what is intolerable to him is that he cannot get rid of himself.[118]

The point is clearly made: Cesare Borgia despairs not because he does not become in his life as overwhelmingly successful as Julius Caesar (chiefly because of the antagonism of Pope Julius II [1443–1513]) but because he cannot shake off his self, which has failed to become as powerful as Caesar.

Now let us look at what Henry makes of this passage. He observes that Cesare Borgia despairs about "this eternal self which in him is the essence of life."[119]

---

[117] Henry, *The Essence of Manifestation*, trans. Girard Etzkorn (The Hague: Martinus Nijhoff, 1973), 676 n. 23.
[118] Kierkegaard, *SUD*, 19.   [119] Henry, *The Essence of Manifestation*, 677.

Borgia suffers not because he failed to control large tracts of Italy but in "the original ontological passivity of Being with regard to itself."[120] Notice that, for Henry (quite unlike Heidegger), the self is eternal. It is worthwhile to pause to see why and how he thinks that this is so:

> As we have already observed, we are not using the verb "to be" on the subject of life – saying, for example, "life is," and then taking this fallacious proposition as a piece of evidence, even though we are speaking of life in human language, which is that of the world – which is precisely that of Being. Life "is" not. Rather, it occurs and does not cease occurring. This incessant coming of life is its eternal coming forth in itself, a process without end, a constant movement. In the eternal fulfillment of this process, life plunges into itself, crushes against itself, experiences itself, enjoys itself, constantly producing its own essence, inasmuch as that essence consists in this enjoyment of itself and is exhausted in it. Thus life continuously engenders itself.[121]

Life is eternal not in the sense of being uncreated but in that it is irreducible to the terms of "the world," which is a state of alienated being, requiring a metaphysics of representation, with beginnings and endings. In his reading of *The Sickness unto Death,* Henry directly appeals to Kierkegaard's sense of eternity: "*The internal structure of immanence, the absolute unity which it encloses and constitutes, this is what Kierkegaard calls eternity, and this rightly so if such a structure is determined by excluding from it the time of transcendence, if positively, the unity which it encloses and constitutes, the interior and living unity of life, cannot be broken.*"[122] Despair is "sickness unto death," as Kierkegaard affirms, because one cannot do away with the self. In Henry's hypnotic prose, despair is eternal "*insofar as the relationship to self subsists in the ego who wishes to break this relationship as the very condition and the essence of the act whereby he wishes to break it, as the condition and the essence of his despair.*"[123] This is not all that *The Sickness unto Death* says or all that Henry says about it. But it suffices to give a sense of the variety of phenomenological views about Kierkegaard. Further thoughts about him will come up in the remaining sections.

I shall end this section by returning to its main theme. Henry's sense of eternity, which he ascribes to Kierkegaard, derives from his understanding of the self-perpetuation of the immanent essence of Life, ζωή not βίος. It is not the neo-scholastic sense of eternity that Heidegger rejects as metaphysical. There is no doubt that Henry covers Kierkegaard's sense of eternity with his own and, in doing so, tends to minimize the scandal of the incarnation by talking of the self-phenomenalizing of phenomenality. Kierkegaard himself maintains that only

---

120 Henry, *The Essence of Manifestation*, 677.   121 Henry, *I am the Truth*, 55.

122 Henry, *The Essence of Manifestation*, 679.   123 Henry, *The Essence of Manifestation*, 679.

Christ, God incarnate, reveals to us the meaning of the eternal, which is the ultimate power of love over death.[124] Indeed, eternity works in and through time, and does so in a twofold manner. As Kierkegaard observes, "The eternal, in the proper sense, continually assigns in possibility just a small part at a time. By means of the possible, eternity is continually *near* enough to be available and yet *distant enough* to keep the human being in motion forward toward the eternal, to keep him going, going forward."[125] Eternity is available in that we can love and be loved here and now; it is far away in that only then can we love God as he ought to be loved and be loved by him in a way that will perfect us. If we can see love from time to time in this life, it is only in the blink of an eye that we can grasp its eschatological fullness for oneself. Kierkegaard may be regarded as having an intentional rapport by way of faith with "Truth crucified"; he may be thought of as leading us back to divine mystery; and he may be regarded by way of the immanence of Life itself in a nonintentional phenomenology. Later on, I shall touch on a fourth possibility.

3 Phenomenology of the Spiritual Life

Kierkegaard steadily maintains, against Gotthold Ephraim Lessing (1729–81), that Jesus's contemporaries had no advantage as regards faith merely because they had personal experience of him. Yet he also maintains that one must become a true contemporary of Jesus through faith in him. It is a view proposed by both Johannes Climacus and Anti-Climacus, as well as over Kierkegaard's own signature; it is indirectly communicated and then directly communicated; and so the importance of becoming a true contemporary of Jesus can hardly be underestimated in the authorship, as well as in the later journals.[126] When Michel Henry considers this motif in his *Material Phenomenology* (1990) he says that it is one feature of what Kierkegaard calls "the strange acoustics of the spiritual world."[127] These acoustics are not those we learn about in physics. As Henry says, "the laws of being in common are not in fact those belonging to things and the laws of perception," and this claim gives Henry an opportunity to continue his long-standing argument with Husserl, a taste of which we have had in earlier sections. Let's begin by trying to understand why they disagree.

---

[124] See, for instance, Kierkegaard, *EUD*, 55.

[125] Kierkegaard, *WL*, 253. More generally, see George Pattison, *Eternal God/Saving Time* (Oxford: Oxford University Press, 2015), esp. ch. 8.

[126] See Kierkegaard, *PF*, 69–70, 90–91, 104–06, 225–26; *WA*, 158–59; *CUP*, vol. 1, 372–74; *PC*, 62–66; and *M*, 287–92.

[127] Henry, *Material Phenomenology*, trans. Scott Davidson (New York: Fordham University Press, 2008), 115. Henry does not give a source for his quotation.

In the fifth of the *Cartesian Meditations* Husserl develops a phenomenology of intersubjectivity by way of defending himself against the charge of transcendental solipsism. Since the sense of "other subjects" is exactly what is in question (and hence the objective world as well), Husserl thinks it is necessary to go further than the transcendental reduction, which would show us only how intentions are related to intentional objects. This additional requirement is a reduction to the "sphere of ownness," which allows one directly to reach pure self-experience in a highly determined sense. I am led back to an originary perception of myself, and only then can I truly discover layers of instituting sense of other subjects as such. But how? I cannot encounter another ego by way of the usual sort of appresentation, making something co-present, for in the sphere of ownness there are no fulfilling presentations: I cannot walk around another ego. Therefore, I must rely on an anterior mode of givenness, one that incipiently belongs to the sphere of ownness.

More particularly, I must have recourse to a special kind of analogy that Husserl calls "pairing." This is a passive association: I vaguely apprehend another ego even before my intentionality begins to act, and the acts of this ego, which differ from my own mental habits, guarantee that it is not a modification of my consciousness. The body of another ego is given to me in the mode "There," not "Here." "It brings to mind the way my body would look 'if I were there.'"[128] It does so in direct empathy, without inference, by reactivating layers of passively instituting sense. We reach back, as it were, to our first intuitive grasping of something similar to ourselves, which is now constituted as pre-given in consciousness. And thus, Husserl concludes, *the assimilative apperception becomes possible* and established, by which the external body over there receives analogically from mine the sense, animate organism, and consequently the sense, animate organism belonging to another 'world,' analogous to my primordial world."[129] Only an ego like my own can be assimilated; there are limits to the recognition of other beings, although Husserl does not specify them. A truly alien being might well strongly resist being incorporated by my ego by way of analogy and empathy.

Henry rejects this account, just as Levinas does. It must be conceded that the Fifth Meditation is not always clear. For example, is the regression to the sphere of ownness really a mode of reduction? Or is it a consequence of reduction that is specified by way of precaution, *viz.* a way of avoiding the mere supposition of constitution occurring beyond my ego?[130] At the same time, it must be noted that

---

[128] Husserl, *Cartesian Meditations: An Introduction to Phenomenology*, trans. Dorion Cairns (The Hague: Martinus Nijhoff, 1977), 118.

[129] Husserl, *Cartesian Meditations*, 118

[130] Husserl does not evoke the "sphere of ownness" in *The Paris Lectures*. It seems likely that the notion came to him by way of conversation with Fink on his return to Freiburg.

Henry does not weigh at all carefully what Husserl says about passive association, apperception, empathy, and the pre-given, and therefore overstates the role that "the laws of perception" play in Husserl's description of intersubjectivity. (Nor does he follow Husserl in his later thinking explored in the *Nachlass*, which sees me as generatively linked to other human beings.) "Analogizing," Husserl says, can "never become an object of perception proper"; it is founded on a perception but also mediated by profiles which cannot be presented directly.[131] That said, Henry takes a clue for proposing an alternate understanding of intersubjectivity by way of Kierkegaard. "Here (*hic*) and there (*illic*)," as Henry understands them, "have nothing to do with the *hic* and *illic* spoken about in the Fifth Cartesian meditation."[132] For Henry, my concrete relation to another person turns on "spiritual acoustics." What does this mean?

It means that the other person is not primarily given to me in noetic–noematic correlation, which, in any case, would yield merely a correlate and not a flesh and blood phenomenon. Before I cognize another person as other than me, even before I see his or her body, I encounter him or her in the mode of affectivity, as *Leib* (flesh), not *Körper* (body), and therefore the other person is conceived invisibly rather than visibly. This is the heart of the difference between the two philosophers. Husserl conceives another sphere of ownness, what Fink calls "the *constitutive becoming of what is existent*," and says that the body of this other ego is given in analogical apperception.[133] For Henry, though, this is consequent on something anterior to all perception, even that presumed in apperception. Self-affective Life is invisibly shared by all egos in a community of pure immanence, prior to any intentional acts. Thus Henry responds to the question "How is the other person given to me?" by way of an appeal to the commonality of immanent Life. He remains within phenomenology by holding fast to the question "How?" And he also brings Kierkegaard into the fold as "the inventor of a radical phenomenology."[134]

Enlisting Kierkegaard's implicit support for nonintentional phenomenology is gained at the expense of taking his remarks on contemporaneity at a quite general level. Let us see what he specifically says about spiritual acoustics in his remarks on Luke 18:9–14, the pericope of the tax collector and the Pharisee in the Temple. "What Scripture says about all tax collectors and sinners, that they kept close to him, whereas the Pharisee in his presumptuous forwardness stood far, far off."[135] The life of the spirit is, Kierkegaard says, "so wondrously . . .

---

[131] Husserl, *Cartesian Meditations*, 112, 119.   [132] Henry, *Material Phenomenology*, 115.

[133] Fink, *Sixth Cartesian Meditation*, 125.

[134] Henry, *Incarnation: A Philosophy of Flesh*, trans. Karl Hefty (Evanston, IL: Northwestern University Press, 2015), 190.

[135] Kierkegaard, "Three Discourses at the Communion on Fridays," *WA*, 131. Also see Kierkegaard, "On the Occasion of a Confession," *TDIO*, esp. 28.

acoustically constructed" and "the ratios of distance" are "so wondrously … established."[136] This religious topology, grounded in concerns about prayer and psychology, is a long way from the phenomenology of intersubjectivity that Henry has in mind. He is solely concerned with a mode of communion with other people, living or dead, that occurs in and through the immanence of self-affecting life. As we have seen in the previous section, Kierkegaard identifies an affectivity in despair; however, he does not generally propose an affective immanence, prior to perception, but rather is concerned with an odd illusion in perception, broadly understood. Two examples will suffice to make this clear.

The first one is well-known. In *Philosophical Fragments* (1844) Johannes Climacus discusses the case of someone who hears the testimony that Jesus is God incarnate and is offended by the scandalous claim. The offense appears to come from a collision of the testimony with his or her cultivated Enlightenment reason yet actually issues from the paradox of an incarnate God. In Kierkegaard's words, the offense comes "from the paradox, even though, making use of an acoustical illusion, it insists that it itself has originated the paradox."[137] The second example occurs in the context of pantheism, which, we are told, is an "acoustical illusion that confuses the *vox populi* and the *vox dei*."[138] One can hear of a union of God and human beings, which is pagan and pantheist, and which Kierkegaard discerns in Martensen's Hegelian-flavored theology, or one can hear of a union of God and a single man, which is Christianity.[139] If we take these two instances of "acoustical illusion" together, we can begin to see a habit of thought in Kierkegaard that can be expanded so that we can detect the outlines of his own phenomenology.

We can see Kierkegaard responding to Ludwig Feuerbach's reductionist thesis in *The Essence of Christianity* (1841) that "Man was already in God, was already God himself, before God became man, i.e., showed himself as man."[140] Not so, says the Dane: This is a pagan illusion.[141] The truth of the matter is that God

---

[136] Kierkegaard, *SUD*, 114.   [137] Kierkegaard, *PF*, 53.

[138] Kierkegaard, *POV*, 123. In a related passage in *PC*, Anti-Climacus speaks of the same situation as an "optical illusion," 81–82. Also see Kierkegaard, *SUD*, 118, and *KJN*, 5, NB 7: 35–37.

[139] For Martensen, Christ is "not one individual among the many but is the absolute individual," which almost sounds Kierkegaardian, yet he adds that Christ "not only reveals the principle of the human race but is this very principle," which is precisely what Kierkegaard objects to in the Hegelian thought of the individual as one with his or her race and his or her times. See Martensen, "The Autonomy of Human Self-Consciousness in Modern Dogmatic Theology," in *Between Hegel and Kierkegaard: Hans L. Martensen's Philosophy of Religion*, trans. Curtis L. Thompson and David J. Kangas, intro. Curtis L. Thompson (Atlanta, GA: Scholars Press, 1997), 113.

[140] Ludwig Feuerbach, *The Essence of Christianity*, trans. George Eliot (New York: Prometheus Books, 1989), 50.

[141] See Kierkegaard, *PF*, 217. Also see Jonathan Malesic, "Illusion and Offense in *Philosophical Fragments*: Kierkegaard's Inversion of Feuerbach's Critique of Christianity," *International Journal of Philosophy of Religion*, 62 (2007), 43–55.

assumed human flesh, became an individual man, not that we humans project our collective consciousness into the heavens and call it "God." We will also find Kierkegaard talking often, especially in his final maturity, of Christendom being an optical illusion. Only if we hear the Gospel properly will we see that Christendom in Golden Age Denmark is nothing like the Christianity proclaimed by Jesus and the apostles. Kierkegaard ponders the question "How does one hear?" And his constant answer is that one must look for the phenomenon not in its echo but in its originating event. Such is the basis of his phenomenology of spiritual life.

Acoustics is the study of sound in all its modes; it includes the investigation of vibration as well as interference and echoes. When Kierkegaard writes of acoustical illusion or spiritual acoustics, he is thinking of echoes rather than interferences and reverberations.[142] For all that, there may well be instances when he prolongs a motif and changes its timbre, as it were, by virtue of his proximity to another thinker, whether one to whom he is sympathetic in some ways (Lessing), one to whom he stands as a critic (Martensen or Bishop Mynster), or one with whom he longs to be close (Christ). Certainly, readers of Kierkegaard are well used to hearing different tones, timbres, pitches, and so on, in the voices of the pseudonyms.[143] We might also wonder if "Kierkegaard" (or "Husserl") when echoing in Henry's prose, is the same author who wrote in Copenhagen or Freiburg. Or is each philosopher an acoustic illusion generated in Montpellier, France? Indeed, would it be more accurate to say that Henry himself increases Kierkegaard's spiritual reverberation when developing material phenomenology?[144] To be sure, there are also vibrations that bounce off Husserl. We are left in no doubt that, as far as Henry is concerned, Husserl is the unwitting victim of an acoustic illusion: The heart of phenomenology may seem to be vivid intuition or intentionality (or the two together) but in reality it is affect. Once we realize that this is so, we are told, we will finally be able to dismiss the problem of solipsism as a red herring that slithers out of Husserl's grasp in the fifth of the *Cartesian Meditations*, affirm community as properly basic, and produce a satisfying phenomenology of intersubjectivity. One part of

---

[142] It needs to be kept in mind that on occasion Kierkegaard speaks of illusion in a positive way, as an ideal. See, for example, *TA*, 67.

[143] See on this issue, Roger Poole, *Kierkegaard: The Indirect Communication* (Charlottesville: University of Virginia Press, 1993), esp. 100–107.

[144] There is a growing body of work concerned to investigate Henry's uses of Kierkegaard. See, in particular, Nicole Hatem, "Le secret partagé: Kierkegaard – Michel Henry, " *Michel Henry. Pensée de la vie et culture contemporaine*, ed. Jean-François Lavigne *et al.* (Paris: Beauchesne, 2006), 195–210, Jeffrey Hanson, "Michel Henry's Problematic Reading of *The Sickness unto Death*," *Journal of the British Society for Phenomenology*, 38: 3 (2007), 248–60, and "Michel Henry and Søren Kierkegaard on Paradox and the Phenomenality of Christ," *International Journal of Philosophical Studies*, 17: 3 (2009), 435–54.

the problem is our relationship with Jesus Christ, which is of profound importance, in different ways, to Kierkegaard and Henry, as we shall see.

Several threads that run through the authorship have already been identified.
I will say a little more about each of them. First, we have seen that acoustic
illusion occurs in religious topology, that is, in the sinner's relationship with
God. As early as *Either/Or* (1843), we hear, through the voice of a pastor in
Jylland (a friend of Judge William's) that this relationship is always perplexed
because "In relation to God we are always in the wrong."[145] It is so even for
a martyr.[146] To expose this illusion, according to Anti-Climacus, is to recognize
that a Christian's overwhelming effort in life must be to become an authentic
contemporary of Jesus Christ, and not merely remain consonant with those
whose lives happen to overlap with one's own. If one does that, one may well
end up a Hegelian (or, for later generations, a Barthian, Tillichian, Rahnerian or
Balthasarian) rather than a Christian. In Christian space, Anti-Climacus insists,
to take one small step away from God is to remove oneself infinitely far from
him.[147] The opposite is also true. As Kierkegaard tells his journal in 1854, "*The
more the phenomenon, the appearance, expresses that it would be impossible
for God to be present, the closer at hand he is.*"[148] The phenomenology of
spiritual life proceeds not only by attending to what appears but also by
investigating the oddities of how the appearing comes to us.

Second, we are alerted to acoustic illusion when considering rhetorical
strategies, sometimes comic or ironic ones, practiced in the authorship, and
this is so in at least three ways. (a) When we approach Christianity in
a theoretical (or philosophical) attitude, the complaints we hear from our reason
about belief in Christ are really effects that come from a hidden cause, *viz.*
hearing the Word of God. (b) Johannes Climacus points to what seems to be an
objective appraisal of Christianity and then indicates that it is an illusion: The
Christian faith must be subjectively appropriated; it is "the existential."[149] (c) It
appears as though the authorship starts from the simple and proceeds to the
complex, passing from aesthetic life to religious life, but in reality it commences
with the complex and proceeds to the simple, all the while staying within the
sphere of religion. Kierkegaard commences his writing career with indirect
communication and only in the second authorship, in a condition of simplicity,
is he able to speak directly.[150]

Third, the problem of mistaking Christendom for Christianity, one of the
refrains of Kierkegaard's entire authorship, especially the second authorship, is

---

[145] Kierkegaard, *EO2*, 339. Also see *UDVS*, 268, 277, 283 and *NB* 17: 92.
[146] Kierkegaard, *UDVS*, 271.   [147] See Kierkegaard, *PC*, 18–19.
[148] Kierkegaard, *KJN*, vol. 10, *KJN* 32: 132.   [149] Kierkegaard, *POV*, 286.
[150] See Kierkegaard, *POV*, 6–7.

a matter of acoustic (or optical) illusion, one steadily, if mildly, practiced by Bishop Mynster throughout his episcopal career and made to reverberate in his successor to be, Martensen, when he declares the old bishop to have been a witness to the truth.[151] When we hear the words "witness to the truth" from Martensen, we are truly hearing a distorted echo of how the Church has understood its martyrs, not to mention Kierkegaard's criticisms of the bishop's watering down of the faith. Of Mynster, Kierkegaard writes in his journal after the bishop's death, "now all that remains is that he has preached Christianity firmly into an illusion."[152]

I will follow the first of these three threads, the issue of being a faithful contemporary of Christ – one's spiritual life, *par excellence* – while being aware of how the other threads sometimes cross over it and even make knots with it. Let us begin at a little distance from this with Johannes Climacus who examines contemporaneity in ethical life. Here, contemporaneity is a task that each of us has; we must strive to unite all the elements of life, from childhood to adulthood, in ourselves; and a thinker must unify imagination, feeling, and understanding. Nothing is to be discarded as one grows. "The true is not superior to the good and the beautiful, but the true and the good and the beautiful belong essentially to every human existence and are united for an existing person not in thinking them but in existing."[153] The point, then, is not to let beauty fade once I become aware of the good, and to take the good as only pre-philosophically containing the truth, or to regard them as objective (or even as transcendentals). Rather, the task is subjectively to appropriate them so that they are all contemporary with me and in me and can abide harmoniously there.[154]

Before affirming this position in the *Postscript*, however, Climacus has already ventured a more existentially demanding valuation of contemporaneity in the *Fragments*. To be historically synchronous with Jesus of Nazareth – the god (ὁ θεός [transl. *ho theos*]), as Climacus has it – merely affords one the opportunity to have empirical knowledge of Jesus. Yet to be an authentic contemporary, to live a spiritual life, is to see Christ in and through faith, to pass from history to eternity by way of "the moment."[155] This act of faith is made "*although it is folly to the understanding and an offense to the human heart*," as Paul says (1 Cor. 1:23).[156] Climacus cites Paul but not Peter who tells us, "Always be prepared to make a defense to anyone who calls you to account

---

[151] See Kierkegaard, *M*, 359.
[152] See Kierkegaard, *M*, 435, as well as 34, 70, 448, 472, 522, 599. Also relevant is *POV*, 41–44. One finds other examples of this reversal of cause and effect. See, for example, *WA*, 35, 79.
[153] Kierkegaard, *CUP*, vol. 1, 348.
[154] Kierkegaard appears to depart from this position from time to time. See, for example, *WA*, 197.
[155] See Kierkegaard, *PF*, 69–70.   [156] See Kierkegaard, *PF*, 102.

for the hope that is in you" (1 Pet. 3:15). In reading Climacus we are hearing more than is ventured in article four of the Augsburg Confession (1530). We might be forgiven for thinking we are hearing someone impressed by the Luther of "The Disputation Concerning the Passage: 'The Word Was Made Flesh'" (1539), with its violent insistence on Christianity's reliance on revelation rather than natural reason (especially Aristotle's sense of reason).[157] The second thesis of the disputation runs: "In theology it is true that the Word was made flesh; in philosophy the statement is simply impossible and absurd."[158] One can maintain that thesis and also say *credo ut intelligam*, but the understanding obtained will have little or no philosophical resonance.

Significantly, Anti-Climacus agrees with the one who comes beneath him in the *scala perfectionis*. The past is actualized, we are told in *Practice in Christianity* (1850), when in an act of faith a single individual makes it necessary for his or her life.[159] Only the single individual, the person who, as we have seen, passes by way of suffering with and for Christ from time into eternity, counts for Anti-Climacus and indeed for Kierkegaard; there are no associations of sacrifice, not even the apostles, for human beings are united in finitude and distinguished individually only in each person's relation to the infinite.[160] The authentic contemporary of Christ believes in his or her Savior's unique claim to divinity and follows him utterly in his degradation and suffering, living in the world in "torment and misery."[161] Discipleship requires one, Anti-Climacus says, to be "the abased one . . . suffering every possible evil, every mockery and insult, and finally to be punished as a criminal."[162] Such is the meaning of *imitatio Christi* for him. Two things are tightly bound together here: a proposal about contemporaneity with Christ and an interpretation of *imitatio Christi*. In order not to get confused, let us separate them. It is easier to do so by taking the second first.

Omnis enim Christi actio, nostra est instruction enim ("Every action of Christ is for our instruction"), Aquinas says, and it is rewarding to reflect on his claim.[163] We can be instructed by pondering Christ's miracles, although we usually do nothing like them ourselves, despite what we are told in John 14:12–14. And we can be instructed by reflecting on his acts of love and his words of

---

[157] See Martin Luther, "The Disputation Concerning the Passage, 'The Word Was Made Flesh'" (1539), trans. Martin E. Lehmann, *Luther's Works*, vol. 38: *Word and Sacrament*, 4, ed. Martin E. Lehmann, gen. ed. Helmut T. Lehmann (Philadelphia: Fortress Press, 1971), 239–77.

[158] Luther, "The Disputation Concerning the Passage, 'The Word Was Made Flesh,'" 239.

[159] Kierkegaard, *PC*, 63–64.

[160] See Kierkegaard, *KJN*, vol. 9, *NB* 28: 71 and *NB* 28: 96. Kierkegaard does not have a lively sense of the election of Christians as a whole to the beatific vision.

[161] See Kierkegaard, *PC*, 107, 170–71, 63.   [162] Kierkegaard, *PC*, 106.

[163] Aquinas, *Quodlibet* 3, q. 5 art. 2.

wisdom. That is, we cannot imitate what renders Christ absolutely singular, that he is fully human and fully divine, and we cannot imitate him in being born without original sin, or in having a death that atones for the sins of the human race (yet see Col. 1:24). These are matters of belief, not objects of possible human imitation. Certainly we can emulate all the human dispositions and deeds of Christ to which the Gospels bear witness; we can place the Father at the center of life, and do our part to bring on the Kingdom, and in doing so we will perform individual versions of being Christian, which is at once being like Jesus (in the ways we can) and being unlike him (since we cannot imitate his absolute singularity). For Anti-Climacus, such *imitatio* must have the same consequences for us as it had for Jesus, so much so that the words "Christian" and "martyr" in effect mean the same thing, "witness to the truth." One must be cautious, though, in this marking of *actio*, especially if one is a Lutheran of any sort, since adherence to *imitatio* might incline believers to think that they might acquire merit through works rather than hold fast to justification by faith alone. Mishearing *imitatio* could endanger one's salvation. Luther, influenced by Bernard of Clairvaux (1090–1153), saw the need to pass from *imitatio operis* to *imitatio mentis*, for the aim of the Christian life is to emulate Christ's faith and humility, not the works of the early saint. Or, as Luther also said, we must practice *conformatas Christi*.[164]

Plainly, if one were to echo Christ's actions, narrowly conceived, there could not be a Christian society of any sort, neither a tradition nor a church.[165] But neither Anti-Climacus nor Kierkegaard is proposing a comprehensive, positive theory of Christians in relation to the State; they are rhetorically opposing the Hegelian *Sittlichkeit* affirmed theologically by Heiberg and Martensen and (in a moderate form) by Bishop Mynster in his sermons.[166] Not that Kierkegaard affirms a spiritual separatism, as one finds in monasticism and in strains of Pietism; for him, in his deepening understanding of *imitatio*, one must suffer invisibly in the world, be "unrecognizable" (with others whose suffering for

---

[164] On this issue see Dietmar Lage, *Martin Luther's Christology and Ethics* (Lewiston, NY: Edwin Mellen, 1990), esp. chs. 3 and 4. Kierkegaard writes of conforming one's mind to one's teacher in *UDVS*, 220.

[165] For Kierkegaard's dismayed view of the establishment of the church at Pentecost, see *KJN*, vol. 9, *NB* 30: 19. It was Martensen's view, as given in the *Berlingske Tidende*, that Kierkegaard's position led him to a version of Christianity without church and tradition. The passage is given by Louis Dupré, in his *Kierkegaard as Theologian: The Dialectic of Christian Existence* (New York: Sheed and Ward, 1963), 193.

[166] For Kierkegaard's private view that a Christian State is un-Christian, even anti-Christian, see *KJN*, vol. 10, *NB* 32: 132, and for the origin of the point I am making, see Merold Westphal, *Kierkegaard's Critique of Reason and Society* (Macon, GA: Mercer University Press, 1987), 22, 105. Kierkegaard's view about the lack of Christianity in Christendom became public in his *Attack on "Christendom"* (1854–55).

Christ is equally hidden) under the terms of Religiousness A as well as B, as Johannes Climacus would add.[167] Of course, we can readily distinguish "Christian" and "martyr" by making the criterion of Christian witness to be complete obedience to the will of the Father, *imitatio mentis*, in which case one might be wholly obedient to God and die "with the cross on," as is the case with a life lived consistent with baptism, if not actually terminated by crucifixion.[168] One must be prepared for a martyrdom like Christ's, but it is not required of us that it happen, or at least not as was all too common under Nero (37–68) and Diocletian (c. 242–311).

To understand how "martyr" is being redefined by Kierkegaard, we must slide back a year, away from Anti-Climacus to H. H., pseudonymous author of "Does a Human Being Have the Right to Let Himself Be Put to Death for the Truth?" (1849). We do not have this right as human beings, we are told; yet Christ has it because he is the truth, and moreover "he came to the world with that *intention*," that is, to die a sacrificial death.[169] Only when people who utterly reject the faith seek to persecute a believer can one accede to martyrdom, H. H. says, and then the martyr can forgive his or her persecutors. Otherwise, in Christendom, one must express one's obedience to God in another fashion and doubtless find that another style of martyrdom comes into focus. Notice that H. H. stresses that Christ *intended*, in eternity, to offer himself as a sacrificial victim on the cross. He may have John 10:18 in mind ("I lay it [my life: ψυχήν (transl. *psuche*)] down of my own accord"). Without a doubt, Johannine Christology allows us to speak of Christ's divine will, and this divine will surely premeditated an atoning sacrifice; but we also need to take note of Jesus's human will. Not that the human will would have been in conflict with the divine will, but Jesus's human will might not have formed any explicit intention to be crucified in order to expiate the sin of the world, or at least might not have formed that intention until a definite moment of his ministry, perhaps even as late as the agony in Gethsemane. It would have been sufficient for the human Jesus to be completely obedient to the will of the Father. There is no reason why more should be expected of a Christian, who has just the one will.

In the same long essay H. H. notes, with a comic element that paradoxically springs from earnestness, that if there is no martyrdom today it is the fault of the potential martyr and not the world.[170] For the potential witness to the truth today

---

[167] See Kierkegaard, *CUP*, vol. 1, 557. For the "unrecognizables," see *TA*, 107–10. I should note that invisible suffering is not a theme developed in the same way by Anti-Climacus, for whom inner suffering is expressed publicly and becomes visible.

[168] Kierkegaard, *UDVS*, 221.

[169] Kierkegaard, "Does a Human Being Have the Right . . .?," *WA*, 65.

[170] For Kierkegaard's explanation of how the comic arises from the earnest, see *SLW*, 366.

does not have "the energy to give the age passion, in this case the passion of indignation, to put him to death."[171] Six years later, in 1855, Kierkegaard goes as far as to assert (and not with his tongue in his cheek) that pastors, especially urban ones, in Denmark are cannibals, living off the early martyrs of the Church.[172] It is no surprise, then, that Kierkegaard privately comes to the defense of both Anti-Climacus and H. H., different as they are in style and stance, arguing that the mode of martyrdom has changed. Nowadays there is "bloodless martyrdom," he tells his journal in 1850, which can be caused through "spiritual overexertion," and he is evidently thinking of his own situation after the *Corsair* affair (1845–46) and his subsequent attack upon the State Church.[173] Unlike those Christians who suffered in the early persecutions, Kierkegaard figures himself as a "long-distance" martyr, someone whose task is to embarrass the comfortable mentality of the crowd and to suffer for it in a protracted way, even if only through public ridicule.[174] Such is the "*Corsair* affair," when Kierkegaard was cruelly lampooned by Peter Klaestrup in his caricatures of him as having a large head and a weak body, and bearing his beloved umbrella whether in rain or shine.

For Anti-Climacus, one can be contemporary twice over, in one's own age and also with Christ's "life upon earth" which, he adds in a paradoxical flourish, is "outside history."[175] In putting things in this way, Anti-Climacus, much like Johannes Climacus, wishes to distance himself from the higher and the lower criticisms, from everything associated with and consequent upon David Friedrich Strauss's *The Life of Jesus Critically Examined* (1835).[176] Genuine Christianity is not open to skeptical investigation by dint of its testimony being 1,800 years in the past. Nor is the Gospel on a par as a text with, say, Homer's *Iliad* or *Odyssey*, which can be illuminated by textual criticism. One must appropriate Christ, but it is less than obvious what this might amount to. It is not a way of encouraging a life of prayer, although to be sure Kierkegaard affirms the need for prayer, and of listening to God more than petitioning him. Rather, it is a matter of the life of Christ, of which prayer was but one feature. Even if one can identify the life of Christ, understood as a sequence of events, from the Gospels, which is very doubtful (for the Gospels are testimonies of belief, not biographies), it is hard at first to see what it would mean to be

---

[171] Kierkegaard, "Does a Human Being Have the Right . . .?," *WA*, 79.

[172] See Kierkegaard, "That the Pastors Are Cannibals, and in the Most Abominable Way," *M*, 323.

[173] Kierkegaard, *KJN*, 7, *NB* 20: 46.

[174] See Kierkegaard, *KJN*, 8, *NB* 21: 69, 6, *NB* 12: 141, *NB* 12: 157.

[175] See Kierkegaard, *PC*, 64.

[176] George Pattison offers a nuanced account of the effects of David Friedrich Strauss on Kierkegaard in his *Kierkegaard and the Theology of the Nineteenth Century: The Paradox and the "Point of Contact"* (Cambridge: Cambridge University Press, 2012), ch. 3.

contemporary with it. One can meditate upon certain events in that life, from birth and childhood to suffering and death, as happens when praying the rosary, or, in a more limited way, by meditating on the passion of Christ by praying the Stations of the Cross. And one can solemnly profess vows of celibacy, poverty, and obedience. All these practices allow one to internalize dispositions of Jesus and events in his life to a greater or lesser degree, but they are all far from Kierkegaard's spirituality.

Perhaps one could become contemporary not with the historical individual, Jesus of Nazareth, but with his spirit as manifested in and through his actions, which could be detached from empirical historical events.[177] More, one could figure this life, the whole span of it and not just the instant of Mary's conception of Jesus, as the incarnation of God. One could be contemporary with Christ by making that spirit proper to oneself, by making it the principle of one's thoughts and moral choices, and not just contemplating it as an image or an ideal.[178] For what is important about Christianity for Johannes Climacus and Anti-Climacus alike is not that its doctrines are representations of the truth, as speculative dogmatic theology would suggest, but that Christ is himself the truth (John 14:6), and that one must (as Anti-Climacus says) reduplicate that truth in one's own life.[179] *Imitatio* and contemporaneity are one in that Christ shows the way to himself. Even if one accepts all of this, there are questions that, niggling as they seem in the face of so much grandeur and passion, need to be answered before the commendation can be put into practice.

The first of these questions is whether there is a spirit that one can associate with Jesus and only with him. One candidate might be compassion (also a distinguishing characteristic of the Buddha, however). Another might be loving self-sacrifice (yet Krishna assumes some of the karma of the Pandavas in a self-sacrificial manner, although not in the sense of taking on "the sins of the world"). Yet another might be being a prophet (although one could say the same of Muhammad). Needless to say, there might be other traits that cannot readily be excluded, including righteous anger and a certain disregard for taking rules and regulations for what they are supposed to regulate, for example Jesus's supposed lack of interest in ritual impurity or for prizing the Sabbath over human distress. It seems difficult to fold these traits into a unity above and

---

[177] It is worthwhile noting Paul Tillich's objection to Kierkegaard's notion of being contemporary with Jesus: If the Christ is the historical Jesus, we cannot be contemporary with him, only with Christ as the Spirit. See Paul Tillich, *A History of Christian Thought from Its Judaic and Hellenistic Origins to Existentialism*, ed. Carl E. Braaten (New York: Simon and Schuster, 1968), 471–72.

[178] See Kierkegaard's hopes for the essay, "Does a Human Being Have the Right to Let Himself Be Put to Death for the Truth?," *KJN*, vol. 6, *NB* 11: 33.

[179] For Johannes Climacus's view, see Kierkegaard, *CUP*, vol. 1, 203.

beyond the specific events that we know of Jesus's life. That there is such a unity is a theological claim. Not that this resolves issues as regards becoming contemporary with Christ, since one could at best only partly appropriate Christ's compassion, loving self-sacrifice, and prophetic role, and even then to different ends.

There is a further objection that needs to be entertained, especially for those more aware of the historical criticism than Kierkegaard could have been. As soon as one says that Christ is "the truth" or "the life," one is not quite contemporary with Jesus of Nazareth, Mary's son. One has brought oneself nearer to Paul's Christ or John's Christ or to the Christ of the Apostle's Creed (and therefore edged closer to N. F. S. Grundtvig [1783–1872] than Kierkegaard would have liked), and in any case one has introduced a gap between the suffering, lowly Jesus who taught the Kingdom and the glorious Savior who one believes to be the eternal Logos, consubstantial with the Father, and whose death has redemptive power.[180] Only if one projects Nicene-Constantinopolitan Christology back into history by way of orthodox belief can the gap be closed; and from the perspective of historical theologians today that is presumably what Kierkegaard does. He thinks he hears a voice in first-century Jerusalem but in fact hears one in late fourth-century Constantinople.

There are other ways of thinking about this situation, which are perhaps more illuminating, and which can be expressed in phenomenological terms. For Henry, of course, one is contemporary with Christ simply by virtue of the self-affectivity of Life. (Needless to say, perhaps, one is also contemporary with Judas, Pilate, and the Roman soldiers who executed Jesus.) One need not go in the direction of a nonintentional phenomenology, however. We might say that Kierkegaard rejects all profiles of Christ, such as offer themselves to the historical critic, precisely because the transcendence of Christ in the philosophical sense of the word (as a body, *Körper*) can distract one from his transcendence in the theological sense of the word (as the absolutely singular God-Man). Christ must be immanent in the individual believer's self, by way of the *imago dei* restored through justification by faith. Only then can one be contemporary with him.[181] So Kierkegaard affirms the need for himself, and all Christians, to perform what we would call a reduction on the Christ who appears in the

---

[180] See Grundtvig's repost to Kierkegaard (without mentioning him by name) in "Elementary Christian Teachings," in Edward Broadbridge and Niels Lyhne Jensen, ed., *A Grundtvig Anthology: Selections from the Writings of N. F. S. Grundtvig, 1783–1872* (Cambridge: J. Clarke, 1984), 135.

[181] For a slightly different sense of being contemporary with Christ, see Joshua Cockayne, *Contemporary with Christ: Kierkegaard and Second-Personal Spirituality* (Waco, TX: Baylor University Press, 2020). Also see Millay, *The Abased Christ: A New Reading of Kierkegaard's "Practice in Christianity"* (Berlin: De Gruyter, 2022), chs. 3 and 4.

Gospels. He is to be led back to the interiority of each individual consciousness and kept secure there. Reduction, here, occurs when there is a definite situation in life in which Christ, God incarnate, becomes thinkable and lovable in one or more of his many profiles. I will return to this leaguing of reduction and contemporaneity in the following section; but now I wish to consider a lost opportunity in Kierkegaard's treatment of Christ as contemporary.

It is surprising that Kierkegaard or one of his pseudonymous authors does not affirm one way by which many Christians seek to make themselves contemporary with Christ, namely through fitting reception of the sacrament of the altar. Luther may reject the Catholic teaching of transubstantiation but he nonetheless reveres the real presence.[182] (The expression hides many views and lives in deep shadow, as is evident to anyone who reads the sacramental theology of John of Paris [c. 1225–1306], Jeremy Taylor [1613–67], or E. B. Pusey [1800–82].) Luther is more precise. He bequeaths the idea of a sacramental union of the body and blood of Christ in, with, and under the forms of bread and wine; and the real presence of Christ is to be found in that union, he believes, and is even to be adored there.[183] In a robust sense, for Lutherans as for Catholics, the sacramental Christ is contemporary with the believer, taken into his or her flesh while the believer receives Grace and is absorbed into Christ.

Kierkegaard embraces this belief, at least in general terms, and lays emphasis on seemly preparation for Communion for the reception of Christ to take place, which includes confession and a rigorous denial of all merit through good works.[184] He ends the second of his "Two Discourses at Friday Communion" (1851) by reminding his audience that Lutherans do not adopt the views of Ulrich Zwingli (1484–1531) or any other of the more radical Reformers. On the altar Christ "gives *himself* to you," we are told,

> the Lord's supper is called communion with him. It is not only in memory of him, it is not only as a pledge that you have communion with him, but it is the communion, this communion that you are to strive to preserve in your daily life by more and more living yourself out of yourself and living yourself into him, in his love, which hides a multitude of sins.[185]

---

182 See Luther, "The Babylonian Captivity of the Church, 1520," trans. A. T. W. Steinhäuser, rev. Frederick C. Ahrens and Abdel Ross Wentz, *Luther's Works*, vol. 36: *Word and Sacrament*, vol. 2, ed., J. J. Pelikan, H. C. Oswald, and H. T. Lehmann (Philadelphia: Fortress Press, 1959), 32–35.

183 See Luther, "The Adoration of the Sacrament (1523)," trans. Abdel Ross Wentz, *Luther's Works*, vol. 36: *Word and Sacrament*, vol. 2, esp. 290–305.

184 Almost all Kierkegaard's remarks on Communion are offered in his own name; the sole exception is the set of comments made by Anti-Climacus, which I consider here.

185 Kierkegaard, "Two Discourses at Friday Communion," *WA*, 187, 188.

The striving that is stressed here is consequent on the reception of the sacrament when one has prepared for it with devout bearing. It is a matter of disciplining oneself to become contemporary with Christ in Communion, of becoming contemporary with him when, on hearing "This is my body" one hears the voice of Christ, and of continuing to be contemporary with Christ in and through words and actions after receiving the sacrament.[186] Eucharist *is* Christ, for Kierkegaard, not a representation of him.[187] If Anti-Climacus thinks the same thing, he does not emphasize the claim.

As Anti-Climacus would be expected to know, the saying of Christ that most disturbed his disciples is this one: "As the living Father [ζῶν πατὴρ] sent me, and I live [ζῶ] because of the Father, so he who eats me will live [ζήσει] because of me. This is the bread which came down from heaven, not such as the fathers ate and died; he who eats this bread will live [ζήσει] for ever" (John 6:57–58). On seeing his disciples' reaction to these words, Jesus asks, "Do you take offense at this? [αὐτοῖς τοῦτο ὑμᾶς σκανδαλίζει]" (John 6:61). They should, Anti-Climacus thinks. For him, however, the incorporation of this stumbling block "in the context of Holy Communion" no longer contains "the possibility of offense"; it has presumably become no more than empty ritual.[188] He rails against those in Christendom who have succumbed to a "fantastic figure of Christ" – Jesus as miracle worker, someone who does not even look lowly and suffering, as he surely did – and relate to this figure only "at the distance of imagination"; his solution is "by having faith," and he affirms the need to be contemporary with Christ, but nowhere thereafter stresses that this contemporaneity already occurs in a privileged mode in the Eucharist or proposes that nominal Christians refresh their devotion to the sacrament, and especially redouble their preparation for receiving it.[189] Anti-Climacus may be for Kierkegaard more of a Christian than Climacus or even Kierkegaard himself, but he is perhaps less of a Lutheran (and more of a Pietist) than Kierkegaard (although he himself had more than a dash of Pietism in his religious character).[190] "At the Communion table," Kierkegaard says, "it is you who are in the debt of sin, you who are separated from God by sin, you who are so infinitely far away."[191] It is the place where it is most important to understand

---

[186] Kierkegaard, *CD*, 271. Also see 261 and 273–74.

[187] See Kierkegaard, "Two Discourses at Friday Communion," *WA*, 187. It should be noted that, on his deathbed, Kierkegaard declined to receive Communion but only because it was to be dispensed by a priest.

[188] Kierkegaard, *PC*, 99.   [189] Kierkegaard, *PC*, 100–102.

[190] See Kierkegaard, *PC*, 281. Yet it must be kept in mind that we never hear Anti-Climacus give an edifying discourse in the context of communion. Also see Christopher B. Barnett, *Kierkegaard, Pietism and Holiness* (Burlington, VT: Ashgate, 2011), esp. ch. 3.

[191] Kierkegaard, *CD*, 299.

spiritual acoustics and thus, for Kierkegaard, a prime site where he could have further bracketed the sedimentations about Christ in Christian culture and, by way of reduction, articulated a phenomenology of the spiritual life.

4 Phenomenology of the Kingdom

Kierkegaard's phenomenology of the Kingdom of God is centered in his meditations on Matthew 6:25–34, in which Jesus tells his disciples not to be anxious about their lives. "Look at the birds of the air," he says, "they neither sow nor reap nor gather into barns, and yet your heavenly Father feeds them. Are you not of more value than they?" (v. 26). Then he adds, "Consider the lilies of the field, how they grow; they neither toil nor spin; yet I tell you, even Solomon in all his glory was not arrayed like one of these" (v. 28). Kierkegaard wrote twice about this passage of Scripture, once in *Upbuilding Discourses in Various Spirits* (March 1846) and again in *The Lily in the Field and the Bird of the Air* (May 1849). Each is an example of Religiousness A, the pursuing of one's natural religious impulse. We can learn about the Kingdom from the illustrations of the birds and the lilies, but we can deepen our understanding of the Kingdom only when we stake our lives on the paradox of the absolutely singular God-Man entering history in the Incarnation and then dying on the Cross.

If we would only contemplate the birds of the air and the lilies of the field, Kierkegaard says in the earlier discourse, we would learn deeply from them. To do this, we must go out into the field, far from cultivated gardens, and behold a lily as though abandoned there. We cannot see lilies grow but we can see *"how they grow"* (hvorledes de voxe).[192] This "how" does not depend on any work that a lily does; on the contrary, its life and beauty are gifts that have been freely given to it and a lily grows in simply accepting these gifts. A lily is silent, and as one contemplates it one begins to compare oneself with it, concluding that, despite one's worries about the world and one's place in it, one lives "exactly in the same sense as the lily, without working and spinning ... more beautiful than Solomon's glory" simply by "being a human being." No other human being could teach as the lily does, and the lesson is learned only because one is far from other human beings and "the worried inventiveness of comparison."[193] Kierkegaard imagines a lily that becomes anxious that there are other flowers, more beautiful than it is; and in its quest to be more like the flowers it imagines, it allows itself to be uprooted and so withers. Then we hear of something similar

---

[192] Kierkegaard, *UDVS*, 162.
[193] On the lily as teacher and imitating the lily, see Wojciech Kaftanski, *Kierkegaard, Mimesis, and Modernity: A Study of Imitation, Existence, and Affect* (London: Routledge, 2022), 221–25.

happening to a dove who longs for more security. Each story underlines what Kierkegaard identifies as "one of the most corrupting kinds of defilement," namely comparison.[194] "It is certainly praiseworthy and pleasing to God that a person sows and reaps and gathers into barns, that he works in order to obtain food," Kierkegaard concedes; "but if he wants to forget God and thinks he supports himself by his labors, then he has worry about making a living."[195] Already, Kierkegaard adumbrates one of his central phenomenological insights, the need to convert one's gaze so as to see God first and foremost in everything one does. To look for God first is to seek the Kingdom; and, as we shall see, this requires us to pass from "the world," source of comparisons and anxiety, to the Kingdom. One must rest in the "how" of a created human being, kept from nothingness not by one's own effort, let alone one's anxiety, but solely by divine love, and then one will be content to be who one is and how one is.

It is worthwhile to pause and see how Kierkegaard both anticipates and differs from Husserl. On the one hand, both philosophers are concerned with a moment of wonder. For Kierkegaard, following the Plato of *Phaedo* 87b–e, it is the wonder of being human and of how one's body clothes one's soul; and for Husserl it is the wonder that noesis correlates with noema. This correlation is discovered, Husserl thinks, in the moment of reduction when one sees phenomena without the need of any philosophical or religious presuppositions. For him, to assume the existence of God or indeed the truth of any Christian doctrine, such as Creation, would remove the freedom that every philosopher requires in order to think well. Yet, for Kierkegaard, the state of pure givenness comes only in and through accepting life as a free gift from God. It is not an assumption but a profound reality hidden by "the world." And in recognizing this, we are led back not to a state without epistemic presuppositions but to the wondrous, basic relation of visible Creation and invisible Creator. For Kierkegaard, there is no more fundamental reality to be found. Philosophical neutrality would be no more than a myth.

As a created being, humans have a special relation with the Creator, since we, and only we, bear the *imago dei*. Just as the Creator is invisible, so too is his image in us. The lily's glory is its visible beauty; ours is our invisible beauty, the life of spirit, which achieves glory in praising the Creator. Again, we are asked to discern what it means to put God first. "The human being and God do not resemble each other directly but inversely; only when God has infinitely become the eternal and omnipresent object of worship and the human being always a worshipper, only then do they resemble each other."[196] If we desire to be like God in ruling others, then we have forgotten God. We may be visible, with

---

[194] Kierkegaard, *UDVS*, 179.　　[195] Kierkegaard, *UDVS*, 177.　　[196] Kierkegaard, *UDVS*, 193.

all the trappings of glory, in our act of governance, but we have lost the glory of being human, which is invisible, and which is embodied in the worship of God. When we praise God we have learned from the birds of the air, which live only in the Now: "the eternal and the temporal touch each other in consciousness or, more correctly, because the human being has consciousness."[197] Neither the lily nor the bird has consciousness, and so cannot represent to itself time to come and concerns for welfare then. To be sure, this capacity to project oneself imaginatively into the future erodes any long-term resting in the eternal we may wish to have; and yet only we are conscious of eternity and have hope of attaining it. Such is one prompt to embrace Religiousness B. We humans have a perfection that the lily and the bird do not have: It is the capacity for work. We have work to do, just as God has (John 5:17), and if one puts God first – that is, seeks the Kingdom first – then we are co-workers with God.

The lily and the bird paradoxically teach us how glorious it is to be human, since to be properly human is to be in relation with God. This is the paradox of learning about Christianity from poetry, from stories (such as Jesus told) of lilies and birds. We learn about being human from that which does not bear the tragic burden of humanity, that we may be eternally lost or saved. The lily and the bird serve only God and do so naturally, and they are therefore perfect up to a point; they lack only the final perfection that comes in freedom. For there can be no love without freedom. Because human beings are free, we may choose to serve God or not to serve him. We have "a choice between God and the world" and it is one that we cannot put aside.[198] The choice does not allow us to have some of God and some of the world; for the peculiarity of our situation as human beings is that God and the world (in the Pauline sense) exclude one another. Citing Matthew 6: 33, Kierkegaard leaves us in no doubt that we "should choose God's kingdom and his righteousness."[199] Where will we find this Kingdom? It is "*within you*," Kierkegaard says, quoting Luke 17:21.[200] We are to look to the *imago dei,* for that is where the eternal touches time. Or, as we shall also be told, we are to cultivate the Kingdom in inwardness.[201]

Let us pause again, first to compare Kierkegaard with Heidegger. In *Der Satz vom Grund,* a course of lectures given in 1955–56, Heidegger reflects on Leibniz's statement of the principle of reason, *Nihil est sine ratione* ("Nothing is without reason"), his principle of all principles, and juxtaposes it with a line from a short poem by Angelus Silesius, the pen name of Johannes Scheffler (1624–77), in his *Cherubinischer Wandersmann* (1657). The line is *Die Rose ist ohne warum; sie blühet, weil sie blühet* ("The rose is without why; it blooms

---

[197] Kierkegaard, *UDVS*, 195.   [198] Kierkegaard, *UDVS*, 206.   [199] Kierkegaard, *UDVS*, 208.
[200] See Kierkegaard, *NB* 12: 180.   [201] Kierkegaard, *NB* 33: 7.

because it blooms"). So there is one thing that is apparently without a reason: the rose. What animates Heidegger is the thought that the principle of sufficient reason, even when stated in what he takes to be its strictest form, *principium reddenae rationis sufficientis*, can be heard in two distinct keys. It can be pronounced "*Nothing* is *without* reason," and it can also be heard as "Nothing *is* without *reason*" so that we discern being in relation with reason.[202] Heidegger invites us to see that the principle (*Satz*) is a qualitative leap (*Satz*). "The principle of reason is a vault into the essence of being in the sense of such a leap," Heidegger says. "We really ought not any longer say the principle of reason is a principle of being; rather, we should say that the principle of reason is a leap into being qua being, that is, qua ground/reason."[203] Now Kierkegaard is not seeking the ground or abyss of beings; instead, he allows the flower to nudge us towards the recognition that we rely wholly upon God for life and for the beauty that is constitutive of being human. In our state of freedom, we must decide for or against God: to love God or to hate him, to put him absolutely first in life or to place him second, which might as well be last in a long series. By the time he was giving his lectures on the principle of reason, Heidegger was no longer a phenomenologist in any narrow sense of the word. But he was perhaps Kierkegaardian in proposing a qualitative leap. Also, he effects a conversion of the gaze, a reduction from one way of regarding the principle to another way of seeing it; and it happens in the blink of an eye. Similarly, Kierkegaard brings us to a point where we must pass from the world to God if we have any stake in the Kingdom.

Before continuing to see more fully what Kierkegaard's implicit reduction means, let us extend the interlude to think a little more deeply about what we are told of the "Kingdom" in Scripture. For Kierkegaard, the Kingdom is within each one of us. If we read the passage he cites with care we see that Jesus says to the Pharisees who are asking him about the Kingdom that the kingdom of God is within you (within your midst) (ἡ βασιλεία τοῦ θεοῦ ἐντὸς ὑμῶν ἐστιν) (Luke 17:21). It is within Jesus and the disciples individually and also in public whenever they appear, but it is not in all human beings and cannot be observed, except, perhaps, glancingly, in the performing of miracles. If the Kingdom can be grasped here and now, it is nonetheless not of this world (John 8:36). More, the New Testament teaches that the Kingdom is breaking in here and now (Matt. 4:17) while it is also to come (Matt. 6:10), that it is weak (2 Cor. 12:9) but also strong (1 Cor. 2:1–5). As taught in the New Testament, the Kingdom is a multi-stable phenomenon, inaugurated by Jesus but to come in fullness only later,

---

[202] Heidegger, *The Principle of Reason*, trans. Reginald Lily (Bloomington: Indiana University Press, 1991), 50.

[203] Heidegger, *The Principle of Reason*, 53.

within groups of people but also beyond them, manifest in human weakness and also in divine strength. Given this, where do we look if we are to seek the Kingdom first?

Certainly, the Kingdom does not appear first in our everyday experience. As children, we open our eyes and look about the world and each of us sees, first, his or her mother, then father, siblings, where one lives, one's neighborhood, one's city, one's country, and so on. Throughout life, when we wake each day, we see the bedroom, the bathroom, the family, the breakfast table, and then where one works. Even if we pray first thing in the morning, we see a Bible or a Prayer Book on a table before we begin. Always, it seems, we see the world first and only then, perhaps, add the Kingdom to our desires in life. Let us listen to how Kierkegaard stresses the anteriority of seeking the Kingdom:

> Seek *first* God's kingdom. This is the sequence, but it is also the sequence of inversion, because that which first offers itself to a person is everything that is visible and corruptible, which tempts and draws him, yes, will entrap him in such a way that he begins last, or perhaps never, to seek God's kingdom. But the proper beginning begins with seeking God's kingdom first; thus it begins expressly by letting a world perish. What a difficult beginning! ... it holds true of seeking God's kingdom that this must be done first; that is unconditionally the only way in which it can be done. The person who thinks of doing it at another time of the day, at some other hour, has not even arrived at the beginning, which after all, is to seek it first. The person who does not seek it first is not seeking it at all, regardless, absolutely regardless of whether he is seeking a penny or millions.[204]

A "sequence of inversion" is the decisive clue to finding the Kingdom. We must turn in the opposite direction to what comes naturally, change the order of things so that we actively seek the invisible rather than the visible; in short, we must upset the normal course of events that is consistently given to us by the world. Kierkegaard quotes Matthew 6:33: "*God's kingdom and his righteousness*," and adds that "the last word describes the first."[205] It is only in seeking purity of heart, and with it, rectitude of life, that one can find the Kingdom. Accordingly, he looks to Matthew 5:8, "Blessed are the pure in heart, for they shall see God" and ponders how to achieve this purity. It is the burden of "An Occasional Discourse," in which Kierkegaard scrupulously examines the thesis "Purity of Heart Is to Will One Thing." He addresses the various barriers to willing one thing, evaluates the cost of such a commitment, and points us to what we must do.

One gains purity of heart only by overcoming double-mindedness, which can occur by willing only the good and doing so in truth, even if this means suffering

---

[204] Kierkegaard, *UDVS*, 210. Also see *NB* 15: 31.   [205] Kierkegaard, *UDVS*, 210.

for the truth.[206] It is this single-minded state that one must attain before confession, and comparison with others will only lead one to delay the act: the "requirement that requires purity of heart is beyond all comparison." Only then does one "win the eternal," that is, one becomes "confirmed in the consciousness that [one] is a single individual and in the task to will one thing in truth."[207] And what is the eternal? It is the Kingdom in the profile of intimacy with God after death. Of course, this view of things obscures other profiles of the Kingdom, its breaking into the world with Jesus, its being established by God on earth, and its self-manifestation in human weakness. One would not expect any historical coordinates of the Kingdom to be pertinent to Kierkegaard, although one might anticipate him countenancing that God acts in strength through human weakness.[208] His commitment is to radical Christianity, an unconditioned single-minded adherence to the good in truth, regardless of the cost.

In the later piece, *The Lily in the Field and the Bird of the Air*, Kierkegaard leaves us in no doubt that seeking the Kingdom first is not a matter of putting it at the start of a list of worthy projects:

> But what does this mean, what am I to do, or what is the effort that can be said to seek, to aspire to God's kingdom? Shall I see about getting a position commensurate with my talents and abilities in order to be effective in it? No, you shall *first* seek God's kingdom. Shall I give all my possessions to the poor? No, you shall *first* seek God's kingdom. Shall I then go out and proclaim this doctrine to the world? No, you shall *first* seek God's kingdom. But then in a certain sense it is nothing I shall do? Yes, quite true, in a certain sense it is nothing. In the deepest sense you shall make yourself nothing, become nothing before God, learn to be silent. In this silence is the beginning, which is to seek *first* God's kingdom.[209]

We do not simply initiate seeking the Kingdom; instead, we must be led back to the opportunity to embrace it. "The beginning," Kierkegaard says directly after the lines just quoted, "is not that with which one begins but that to which one comes, and one comes to it backward." We must pass from our everyday experience of the world to standing nakedly before God. "The beginning is this art of *becoming* silent" in fear and trembling before God Almighty. In doing so, one learns that prayer is not speaking to God or even overhearing oneself speak to him but attentively listening to him and being transformed in and

---

206 Kierkegaard, "On the Occasion of a Confession: Purity of Heart Is to Will One Thing," *UDVS*, 120.
207 Kierkegaard, "On the Occasion of a Confession," *UDVS*, 152.
208 Yet see Kierkegaard, *CD*, 130.
209 Kierkegaard, "The Lily in the Field and the Bird of the Air," *WA*, 10–11.

through that act. In an instant that cannot be programmed, one begins life again, from the very beginning. The lily teaches us the proper mode of access to the Kingdom: a prayerful silence in which no thought, no plea, is represented. In returning to this state, in finding genuine firstness, one cannot plausibly think that anything else would come second or third. If one has God, one has everything there is. But there is more to say about this situation and philosophical approaches to it, whether phenomenological or analytic.

It will have become apparent over the course of these chapters that phenomenology can be developed along philosophical lines, such as Husserl's and Heidegger's, and that it can also be extended along theological lines. The former approach prizes a situation without presuppositions: One receives only that which is given to one in lively intuition (Husserl) or one describes the world without reference to God (Heidegger). In these situations religious experience, and theological reflection on it, is inevitably translated into philosophical terms. An example is found when David J. Kangas (1964–2016), as careful a reader of Kierkegaard, and as well-attuned to phenomenology, as one might hope to find, reads the very texts that have interested us in this chapter and, reflecting on *Eftergivenhed* (roughly: pliancy) concludes:

> The creature must become pliant, absolutely pliant, to what they're undergoing; must take the measure of reality and itself from what it is undergoing; and not attempt to gain mastery of the event by reframing it as a "moment" in a larger project. "God" is here is placeholder for the affirmability of reality outside contexts of meaning. Reality can be affirmed without that affirmation being grounded in a meaning: that is precisely what *Eftergivenhed* accomplishes.[210]

What is striking here is the translation of religion to philosophy marked in the move to interpret God as a "placeholder" for "the affirmability of reality outside contexts of meaning." *The Lily in the Field and the Bird of the Air* begins with a prayer to God the Father, as does "What We Learn from the Lilies in the Field and from the Birds of the Air." It is implausible to think that Kierkegaard considered "God" to be merely a placeholder for anything else; and one must therefore look with skepticism on any quest to find a "philosophical meaning" of Kierkegaard's religious discourses if that meaning is purchased at the cost of excluding its religious significance.

Similarly, one finds in analytical philosophy a tendency to see Kierkegaard as simply unreasonable in how he figures the demands of Christianity. As we have seen, the point of the single-mindedness that Kierkegaard commends is that the

---

[210] David J. Kangas, *Errant Affirmations: On the Philosophical Meaning of Kierkegaard's Religious Discourses* (London: Bloomsbury, 2018), 168.

Kingdom is heterogeneous with the world: Purity of heart occurs, if it does, in an everyday moment that touches a wholly other order, the eternal, than in one's everyday dealings with the world and in the world. And it is in an awareness of the anteriority of this spiritual order that we can understand that the Kingdom is to be sought before anything else. We might say, following the philosophy of priority elaborated by Sébastian Izquierdo (1601–81), that for Kierkegaard eternity is absolutely prior to both nature and the world with respect to value: There can never be a comparison adequate to what is offered by eternal life in the Kingdom.[211] Now one might respond to this by saying, as Philip Quinn (1940–2004) does in quite another context, that Kierkegaard "has a proclivity for pushing things to extremes from which we would do well to recoil."[212] Reasonable and careful, Quinn worries that Kierkegaard's religious intensity, presumably manifest in Religiousness B, prompts him to believe that he has a "providential mission to overturn the Established Church" and that it poses a danger for ethics and needs to be balanced by other factors. Quinn writes, "I consider relinquishing a certain amount of rational control over one's life in order to allow space in it for some disunity, either psychic or narrative, to be a price worth paying to purchase opportunities to pursue plural but potentially conflicting goods if they are great enough." Kierkegaard's view of first seeking the Kingdom would risk, or more than risk, "oversimplification within our ethical lives," including, for example, breaking his engagement with Regine Olsen.[213]

One difficulty here is that Kierkegaard saw that the Danish Church, both in its episcopacy and in its State theologians, was most certainly not seeking the Kingdom; rather, it was content to make Denmark into a pallid earthly version of the Kingdom, a moral commonwealth.[214] But that is Christendom, not Christianity; and it is incumbent on all Christians to criticize the Church when it preaches or teaches Christianity into an illusion. Another, more significant, difficulty is that the Kingdom is not simply ethical (despite what we heard Levinas say on the matter in the second section): It is also a matter of the creature's worship of his or her Creator, and if this is an absolute priority it cannot be compared with others so as to generate plural goods. They would be secondary. One is commanded to love "the Lord your God with all [ὅλης] your heart, and with all [ὅλης] your soul, and with all [ὅλης] your mind, and with all

---

[211] See Brian Embry, "Sébastian Izquierdo's (1601–1681) Theory of Priority," *Journal of the American Philosophical Association*, 4: 4 (2018), 491–509.

[212] Philip L. Quinn, "Unity and Disunity, Harmony and Discord: A Response to Lillegard and Davenport," in John J. Davenport and Anthony Rudd, ed., *Kierkegaard after MacIntyre: Essays on Freedom, Narrative, and Virtue* (Chicago: Open Court, 2001), 327.

[213] Quinn, "Unity and Disunity," 330.

[214] See, for example, Kierkegaard, *NB* 9: 68, *NB* 11: 87 and *NB* 25: 50.

[ὅλης] your strength." Yet this is not all. One is also commanded, "You shall love your neighbor as yourself" (Mark 12:30–31). So when we are told, "seek first [πρῶτον] his kingdom and his righteousness" (Matt. 6:33), we are enjoined, Kierkegaard thinks, to seek purity of heart, which will bring about not only what we need in order to survive in this life but also moral rectitude in dealing with oneself and others.

We must not confuse Kierkegaard's particular decisions, based upon his personal circumstances and his psychology, for example not to marry Regine and thus to forego having children, with the generality of the thesis ("Purity of heart is to will one thing") that he advocates. The quest for the Kingdom is anterior to our conduct of our ethical lives, absolutely prior in worth to all speech and all actions, even if we have spoken and acted for decades before turning to the Kingdom; it occurs apart, in an unpredictable instant of silent prayer that leads one back to the asymmetric relation of Creator and creature, and pursuing it does not mean that we cannot marry and have children, as Quinn fears, or indeed pursue a variety of goods. Elsewhere, Kierkegaard is clear that prayer involves possibility, "because the being of God means that everything is possible."[215] One such possibility is marriage. The care of one's spouse and offspring, in worldly terms, cannot be compared in terms of worth with one's own salvation or the salvation of one's spouse and children. Salvation is not one good among others; it is an absolute value for each person. But one cannot conclude that, if one is married, the quest for salvation is at odds with love for spouse and offspring: One is commanded to love both God and neighbor, and one's family are the first neighbors one encounters on any given day.

It is in an instant, in which time touches eternity, when as a solitary individual one encounters God in fear and trembling, and begins to know him as a contemporary; and in that instant, that blink of an eye, one undergoes a reduction from "world" to "Kingdom," just as one does when hearing a parable.[216] If we return to Husserl's generative phenomenology, mentioned in the first section, we might adopt and adapt its terms and say that when this moment occurs, one's home world is overturned, and one realizes that, amazingly, one has never actually lived in one's true home world.[217] For a time, one may experience a vertiginous sense of homelessness. Now one must learn to live with Christ, the Truth, to make *him* one's contemporary; but how is one to do that? At first, it may be difficult, since Christ and his Kingdom cannot be simply integrated into "the world"; it is challenging enough to

---

[215] Kierkegaard, *SUD*, 40.   [216] See Kierkegaard, *NB* 2: 17 and *NB* 3: 77.
[217] Again, I refer to Steinbock, *Home and Beyond*.

assimilate them into one's natural ways of being, since Christianity often rubs against nature. A new community must be found, and it may well take considerable time to discover one that feels like home. While still speaking English, French, or Danish, one must also internalize a new language, that of the New Testament and its heritages. Even if one has objectively known its vocabulary – "forgiveness," "Grace," "mercy," "sin," "sacrifice," "prayer," and all – from childhood, one has now to make it fully one's own. Its stories, from the parables of Jesus to the lives of the saints and far beyond, become increasingly familiar, and many of these too are appropriated. One must learn to balance one's new language against the prayerful silence that is required when listening to God. Gradually, one begins to inhabit another tradition, another generative community of witnesses to the truth, with its own liturgical gestures, practices, and idioms.

One begins to accept new norms and, in doing so, to let others fade. For a while, perhaps a very long time, one lives within a twofold narrative, that of the world and that of the Kingdom, and even when aspects of the generative community of the world become increasingly alien the whole never becomes unfamiliar.[218] It attracts, whether darkly or brightly. One might need to be led back from "world" to "Kingdom" more than once, perhaps by other means, and one might migrate from one faith community to another. At one end of the spectrum, the conservative, "world" and "Kingdom" will be starkly opposed: Christ will be seen as a "sign of contradiction" (Luke 2:34). At the other, liberal end of the spectrum, "world" and "Kingdom" will associate with one another.

For Kierkegaard, Christendom appeared unnervingly alien, an illusion of Christianity, and his task in his latter days was to denounce it as an inauthentic home world for Christians, to show that it was in truth an alien world subsisting on the authentic generative world of faith. Yet the Kingdom is always, to some extent, beyond one's comprehension no matter how long or how firmly one takes oneself to have been adopted into it; it is multi-stable, as we have seen, and irreducibly mysterious; while the world around us appears stable, commonsensical, ordered, even if at times it also becomes incomprehensible because one's hopes and values have changed. For the one who has crossed over, there is a distinct sense in which one can no longer understand the deep assumptions and narratives of one's former world; they have their own depths, to be sure, and perhaps their own reasons and even their own appeal as well, but they have lost their familiarity, naturalness, and inevitability. The mode of being that is affirmed in the old world no longer makes sense, can hardly be regarded as satisfying, let

---

[218] See Kierkegaard, *NB* 19: 18.

alone fulfilling. "They" see human beings as being-directed-unto-death, but now "we" see ourselves as being-attracted-to-God. Things have changed: One's gaze has been converted. One no longer asks what Christianity is, or whether it is true; rather, one asks how to gain deeper access to it. For having found a new home does not eliminate a sense of homelessness, as Kierkegaard himself knew. Christians are never fully at home in this life.

Afterword

Is Kierkegaard a phenomenologist? Yes, if we read him in terms of the context of discovery, not the context of justification. Similar cases, although with very considerable variations, can be found in many thinkers and writers before Husserl, and even before Descartes. Even so, we should not think that he is a phenomenologist in anything like the manners that Husserl and the younger Heidegger are. For one thing, he cannot be expected to use the vocabulary that one associates with twentieth- and twenty-first-century phenomenology, especially that of reduction. For another thing, although he pursues a philosophical approach to phenomenology from time to time, his concern as a religious author also takes a theological path. For him, one is led back from "world" to "kingdom" not only by way of parables but also by way of what he calls "the moment."

Abbreviations

CA	*Concept of Anxiety: A Simple Psychologically Orienting Deliberation on the Dogmatic Issue of Hereditary Sin*, ed. and trans. by Howard V. Hong and Edna H. Hong, Kierkegaard's Writings, 8 (Princeton, NJ: Princeton University Press, 1980).
CD	*Christian Discourses: The Crisis and a Crisis in the Life of an Actress,* ed. and trans. by Howard V. Hong and Edna H. Hong, Kierkegaard's Writings, 17 (Princeton, NJ: Princeton University Press,1997).
CUP	*Concluding Unscientific Postscript,* ed. and trans. by Howard V. Hong and Edna H. Hong, Kierkegaard's Writings, 12.1 (Princeton, NJ: Princeton University Press, 1992), vol. 1.
EO1/EO2	*Either/Or, Part I*, and *Either/Or, Part II*, ed. and trans. by Howard V. Hong and Edna H. Hong, Kierkegaard's Writings, 3 and 4 (Princeton, NJ: Princeton University Press, 1987).
EUD	*Eighteen Upbuilding Discourses*, ed. and trans. by Howard V. Hong and Edna H. Hong, Kierkegaard's Writings, 5 (Princeton, NJ: Princeton University Press, 1990).
FT/R	*Fear and Trembling* and *Repetition*, ed. and trans. by Howard V. Hong and Edna H. Hong, Kierkegaard's Writings, 6 (Princeton, NJ: Princeton University Press, 1983).
KJN	*Kierkegaard's Journals and Notebooks*, 11 vols., ed. by Bruce H. Kirmmse *et al.*, trans. by Alastair Hannay *et al.* (Princeton, NJ: Princeton University Press, 2007–2020).
M	*"The Moment" and Late Writings*, ed. and trans. by Howard V. Hong and Edna H. Hong, Kierkegaard's Writings, 23 (Princeton, NJ: Princeton University Press, 1998).
NB	*Kierkegaard's Journals and Notebooks*, ed. Bruce H. Kimmse *et al.* (Princeton, NJ: Princeton University Press, 2007–).
PC	*Practice in Christianity*, ed. and trans. by Howard V. Hong and Edna H. Hong, Kierkegaard's Writings, 20 (Princeton, NJ: Princeton University Press, 1991).
PF	*Philosophical Fragments* and *Johannes Climacus*, ed. and trans. by Howard V. Hong and Edna H. Hong, Kierkegaard's Writings, 7 (Princeton, NJ: Princeton University Press, 1985).

POV   *The Point of View*, ed. and trans. by Howard V. Hong and Edna
             H. Hong, Kierkegaard's Writings, 22 (Princeton, NJ: Princeton
             University Press, 1998).

SLW   *Stages on Life's Way,* ed. and trans. by Howard V. Hong and Edna
             H. Hong, Kierkegaard's Writings, 11 (Princeton, NJ: Princeton
             University Press, 1989).

SUD   *The Sickness unto Death*, ed. and trans. by Howard V. Hong and
             Edna H. Hong, Kierkegaard's Writings, 19 (Princeton, NJ:
             Princeton University Press, 1980).

TA   *Two Ages: The Age of Revolution and the Present Age,
             A Literary Review*, ed. and trans. by Howard V. Hong and Edna
             H. Hong, Kierkegaard's Writings, 14 (Princeton, NJ: Princeton
             University Press,1978).

TDIO   *Three Discourses on Imagined Occasions*, ed. and trans. by
             Howard V. Hong and Edna H. Hong, Kierkegaard's Writings,
             10 (Princeton, NJ: Princeton University Press, 1993).

UDVS   *Upbuilding Discourses in Various Spirits,* ed. and trans. by
             Howard V. Hong and Edna H. Hong, Kierkegaard's Writings,
             15 (Princeton, NJ: Princeton University Press, 1993).

WA   *Without Authority,* ed. and trans. by Howard V. Hong and Edna
             H. Hong, Kierkegaard's Writings, 18 (Princeton, NJ: Princeton
             University Press, 1977).

WL   *Works of Love*, ed. and trans. by Howard V. Hong and Edna
             H. Hong, Kierkegaard's Writings, 16 (Princeton, NJ: Princeton
             University Press, 1995).

Acknowledgments

I would like to thank Rick Anthony Furtak for inviting me to contribute this Element to his series and for reading over a fair draft of the manuscript before it was submitted. Thomas J. Millay read the same draft and made many very useful comments: The Element has been improved by his kind attentions. David Beadle, my research assistant, worked tirelessly to find quotations and check citations and produced the table of abbreviations. Without his assistance, the Element would have taken months longer to complete. Christina Gschwandtner and Carl Scerri generously assisted me in locating references: My warm thanks to each of them. Gavin Flood, Phil Gates, Walter Jost, and Steven DeLay each read the manuscript with care, and the Element is better for their kind attention. My wife, Sashanna Hart, read the whole manuscript and asked many pertinent questions. I am thankful to Stanley Hauerwas and Kavin Rowe for reading the manuscript and for their encouragement. An earlier version of Section 3 was given as the 2015 annual Kierkegaard Lecture at the American Academy of Religion (AAR) in Atlanta and a version of it was published in *Analecta Hermeneutica*, 8 (2016). My thanks to the Søren Kierkegaard Society USA for the honor of inviting me to give the lecture and for the journal to allow me to use the material as the basis of new work.

For Sashanna

Philosophy of Søren Kierkegaard

Rick Anthony Furtak

Colorado College

Rick Anthony Furtak is Associate Professor of Philosophy at Colorado College and past President of the Søren Kierkegaard Society (for calendar years 2013–2014). He has published two books and over twenty essays on Kierkegaard's work, including *Wisdom in Love: Kierkegaard and the Ancient Quest for Emotional Integrity* (2005) and *Kierkegaard's 'Concluding Unscientific Postscript': A Critical Guide* (2010), along with the co-edited *Kierkegaard and the Poetry of the Gospel* (2025). He has contributed to each of the *Cambridge Critical Guides* on Kierkegaard's writings, and has dozens of other philosophical and poetic publications. He is also an Editorial Board Member for *New Kierkegaard Research* and founding Book Series Co-Editor for *Bloomsbury Studies in Philosophy and Poetry*. His other recent books include *Love, Subjectivity, and Truth* (2023).

About the Series

This series offers concise and structured introductions to all aspects of the philosophy of Søren Kierkegaard. Some Elements are organized around particular themes, while others are devoted to specific Kierkegaardian texts. Both well-established and emerging scholars contribute to the series, combining decades of expertise with new and different perspectives.

For EU product safety concerns, contact us at Calle de José Abascal, 56–1°,
28003 Madrid, Spain or eugpsr@cambridge.org.